Cryptocurrency Investing Bible: Your C

Step-by-Step Game Plan for Massive Long-Term Profits

in the World's Fastest Growing Market

This book contains 4 Manuscripts:

- What the World's Best Blockchain Investors Know - That You Don't

- 13 More Coins to Watch with 10X Growth Potential in 2018

- 10 Biggest Trading Mistakes Newbies Make - And How to Avoid Them

- What You Need to Know About Taxes to Avoid a Nasty Surprise from The IRS

By Stephen Satoshi

Contents

Financial Disclaimer:

I am not a financial advisor, this is not financial advice. This is not an investment guide nor investment advice. I am not recommending you buy any of the coins listed here. Any form of investment or trading is liable to lose you money.

There is no single "best" investment to be made, in cryptocurrencies or otherwise. Anyone telling you so is deceiving you.

I am not affiliated with any coin or cryptocurrency mentioned in this book.

There is no "surefire coin" - one again, anyone telling you so is deceiving you.

With many coins, especially the smaller ones, the market is liable to the spread of misinformation.

Never invest more than you are willing to lose. Cryptocurrency is not a get rich quick scheme.

Affiliate Disclaimer:

Like cryptocurrency, I too believe in transparency and openness, and so I am disclosing that I've included certain products and links to those products on in this book that I will earn an affiliate commission for any purchases you make. Please note that I have not been given any free products, services or anything else by these companies in exchange for mentioning them in this book.

Accuracy Disclaimer:

All prices and market capitalizations are correct at the time of writing. Price and market cap information is sourced from coinmarketcap.com. All information in this eBook was derived from official sources where possible. Official sources meaning literature that is publicly available, provided by the development team for each cryptocurrency or company such as a company website or GitHub page. At the time of writing, some of the information is not available in English from official sources. In this case some of the information included in this eBook was obtained from unofficially translated whitepapers. Unofficially meaning either via computer translation, or third party human translation.In this case some of the information included in this eBook was obtained from unofficially translated whitepapers. Unofficially meaning either via computer translation, or third party human translation.

Cryptocurrency Market Cap 2017

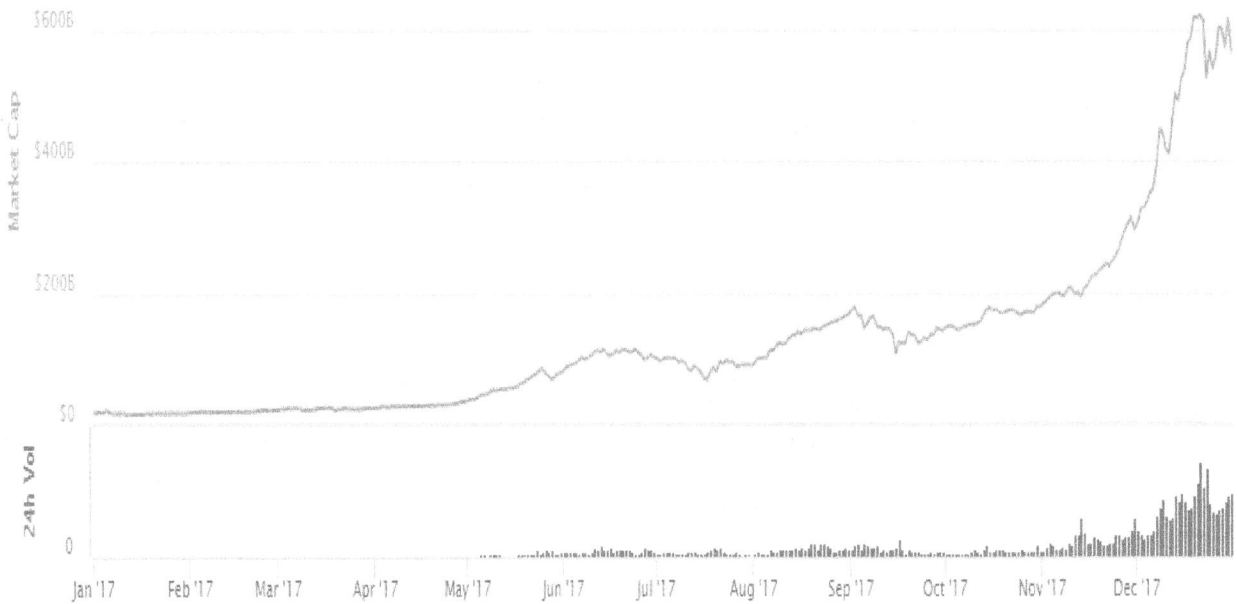

Total Market Capitalization

Cryptocurrency: What the World's Best Blockchain Investors Know - That You Don't

By Stephen Satoshi

Introduction - The current cryptocurrency playing field

Today the market cap of the cryptocurrency market stands at $560 billion. For the record that's up around 3000% from January 1st 2017.

We saw Bitcoin, the original cryptocurrency, hit highs of $20,000.

Then came the rise of Ethereum, the revolutionary smart contract and decentralized application platform, went from $9 to over $1000.

And then there were lesser reported success stories, like that of Neo, formerly known as Antshares, the Chinese smart contract token that rose from less than $1 to over $100 in the space of 7 months. Then there was that of Dogecoin, a microtransaction platform and tipping coin, which was started as a fun inside joke reached a market cap of over $800 million.

We even saw bizarre stories such as that of a Turkish amateur soccer team buying a player from a rival for 0.0524 Bitcoin, which was around $520 at the time the transfer occurred.

It doesn't take a genius to see that 2017 was a big year for cryptocurrencies. This was the year that finally hammered home that they are here to stay.

So now the chaos is temporarily over, let's take a step back, and examine where the market is going heading forward.

You see this influx of money is not just limited to cryptocurrency, we have to consider the blockchain technology behind it, and it's wide reaching ramifications for not only financial markets but also society as a whole.

Major firms like IBM, Walmart and Samsung are spending billions of dollars in blockchain research, or in developing their own blockchain solutions. A video played at the Davos World Economic Forum, attended by some of the world's most powerful figures, including US President Donald Trump, was titled "Blockchain is Coming and It Could Save Lives"

What's even more exciting is that we're still very much in the initial stages of the blockchain boom. For comparison, the global stock market cap for comparison is $80 **trillion,** this alone demonstrates that we are still in the extremely early stages of adoption. For further comparison, the cryptocurrency market is still smaller than the stock exchanges of countries like Taiwan and Spain. Needless to say, we've still got a long way to go, and in terms of an investment standpoint, there's a lot more money to be made.

That doesn't mean there won't be periods of turbulence, 2018 is off to a rocky start, and we're likely to see a significant pullback that could last as long as the first 3-6 months of the year. That's OK if you're a long term believer in the technology, but if you're looking for a get rich quick scheme, you probably aren't going to be too happy.

Even so, there are still huge gains to be made in the cryptocurrency market, you just have to know where to look.

If all else fails, remember the timeless phrase "bulls make money, bears make money, pigs get slaughtered."

What this book is not

This book is designed as a guide to help you become more informed in how the boom in Bitcoin, other cryptocurrencies and blockchain technology is affecting to wider financial market as a whole. How it affects different sectors of the market, and the correlation between cryptocurrency and blockchain.

This is not a blind recommendation to buy all stocks, ETFs or managed funds with "blockchain" in their name. Doing so would be a great way to lose money very quickly.

As with all my books, I am not a financial advisor, and I am not advising you to buy any of the stocks, or cryptocurrencies listed in this book.

As with any investment, never invest more than you can afford to lose.

Separating cryptocurrency from blockchain technology

So if you have a basic understanding of blockchain technology, you'll be fully aware that without it, there is no basis for cryptocurrency to exist. Blockchain gives us the ability to create indisputable, public ledgers, which everyone can see, but no single person can control. These ledgers can verify financial transactions, and this is what gives cryptocurrency the ability to have inherent value, and allows people to have trust in the system, without having to rely on third party institutions like banks.

This has led to some calling blockchain "The Backbone of Finance's Entire Future". And a survey by the World Economic Future estimates that 10% of the world's GDP will be stored on a blockchain ledger by 2025 - that's roughly $10 trillion if we use 2018 numbers.

However, blockchain technology has far wider reaching ramifications than merely a cryptocurrency facilitator. From smart contract platforms, all the way to having the ability to verify federal election results. The ramifications stretch across hundreds of different industries and have the ability to change society for the better. This is precisely why giant corporations like Microsoft, Tesla and Walmart are spending billions of dollars on blockchain research and blockchain protocols of their own.

The key takeaway from blockchain technology is that of trust. Due to the fact that information recorded on a blockchain cannot be altered, there is an indisputable record of all transactions that have taken place. These transactions don't have to be strictly financial in nature. They can be used to verify who owns certain assets, to optimize supply chain processes (more on that later) and to identify tampering and fraud.

By being able to identify exactly which industries and companies are becoming early adopters of blockchain, we can begin to see just exactly where growth areas will begin to emerge.

Why are so many "experts" predicting Bitcoin's downfall?

For as long as cryptocurrency has existed, we've been inundated with news articles professing the "death" of Bitcoin. What these experts neglect to tell you is that they've already predicted the so-called "death" of Bitcoin over 200 times in the past 5 years.

The first mainstream media article of this type was back in January 2011 when Forbes published an article "So that's the death of Bitcoin then". The Huffington post called Bitcoin a "hoax" during this time.

In fact, there are now so many Bitcoin obituaries, that there's even a website dedicated to them. https://99bitcoins.com/obituary-stats/ generously lists 245 different predictions of the death of Bitcoin. There were even predictions as far back as 2010, needless to say, those naysayers have been proven wrong time and time again.

Bitcoin has overcome a number of hurdles up to this point. From a 68% drop in value in mid 2011, to the Mt. Gox exchange hacks of 2014 and the misinterpreted rumors of China banning cryptocurrency in 2017.

Mainstream adoption for Bitcoin and other cryptocurrencies continues to grow year-on-year, in fact at the beginning of 2018 there were less than 10 countries worldwide that do not recognize Bitcoin as having value (note, this differs from Bitcoin transactions being legal in said country).

So why do so many different news outlets predict the downfall of Bitcoin? Simply put, the vast majority of mainstream news outlets have ZERO experience with cryptocurrency. Even their financial reporters are outsiders when it comes to blockchain technology and its implications. Yes, that includes traditional stock market analysts, many of whom are no more clued in than the average investor when it comes to this new asset class.

One of the major reasons for this is that at its core, Bitcoin is a decentralized financial model, which of course disrupts the traditional banking system. Therefore the voices of this system, a system that has made them more money than they could ever know what to do with, have often spoken out against anything that they perceive as a threat to their status quo.

Arguably the biggest critic of Bitcoin has been Jamie Dimon, the CEO of JP Morgan Chase. Previously calling Bitcoin a "fraud" and "worse than tulip bulbs". Dimon also threatened to fire any staff member who traded bitcoins.

It is only now, from around mid 2017 onwards that we've started seeing some level of institutional adoption of cryptocurrency. This is because banks and other large financial institutions have worked out a way that they can profit from cryptocurrencies themselves. However as we saw in early 2018, banks would prefer to do this at a lower price point, which has been a major factor in the depressed cryptocurrency prices we've seen at the beginning of 2018.

I'll be explaining this more in depth later on in the book, but I believe that we'll be seeing less and less "death of Bitcoin" predictions as we move forward.

How will blockchain technology affect banks?

While there are some who predict that blockchain technology will lead to the downfall of the entire banking system as we know it, it's unlikely that this will be the case.

It's true that in the original Bitcoin whitepaper, there was revolutionary language talking about doing away with the need for financial institutions. Many cryptocurrency enthusiasts fervently discuss "the original Bitcoin vision" when debating about the use of traditional banks. This has also led to many people on the ideological side of cryptocurrency dismissing coins like Ripple (XRP) which help facilitate payments in the banking sector.

However, banks themselves have now begun to integrate blockchain into their own business model. First, there is the Ethereum Enterprise Alliance, a group of 200 organizations who are testing Ethereum blockchain solutions in a wide variety of industries. This group includes some mega banking corporations such as Credit Suisse and JP Morgan Chase.

Mega banks are developing their own blockchain solutions. Goldman Sachs for example now has a page dedicated to blockchain on its website, aimed at educating customers about the potential uses of the technology.

There's also the question of how central banks will utilize blockchain technology, and even if they will create their cryptocurrencies. More on that subject later on in the book.

It should be noted that there is a specific sub-sector of cryptocurrency that banks do not favor, namely privacy based coins like Monero, ZCash and Aeon. These coins do represent a real threat to banking by offering completely anonymous transactions and essentially allowing users to be their own bank. This has led to some calling Monero, the most widespread and highest market cap privacy coin, "Swiss bank 2.0"

How similar is this to the DOTCOM boom?

Detractors of blockchain technology are eerily similar to those who said the same thing about the internet in the early to mid 90s. As AOL CEO Steve Case said "The conventional wisdom was that the internet would always be limited to hackers and hobbyists"

Then there is the famous 1995 Newsweek article written by Clifford Stoll entitled "Why the Web won't be Nirvana" with now laughable claims such as "The truth is no online database will replace your daily newspaper." Stoll, a widely respected astronomer also went on to called the idea of ecommerce "baloney". Needless to say, he missed the mark by just a little bit.

The point of re-visiting these claims is that we are still in the very early stages of cryptocurrency and blockchain technology. Even experts in other technological fields have very little idea of how it works, and the wider ramifications for society at large. Therefore we are liable to misinformation, hot takes and all round confusion.

These similarities also go the other way though. Just like many companies saw their stocks rise by putting ".com" at the end of their name. We are seeing the same effect with blockchain.

For example, in October 2017, On-Line PLC renamed itself to On-Line Blockchain PLC, and saw its shares jump 394% in less than 24 hours.

Another example was seen In December 2017, when a microcap company called Long Island Iced Tea Corp simply changed its name to Long Blockchain and saw its stock rise 289% in just over a week. The company, which sells non-alcoholic beverages and at the time of writing has no blockchain agreements in place.

Examples like these go to show, that there may be a "bubble-like" effect. Not all of these projects will succeed. In fact, over 90% of ICOs will fail, and I would estimate the same figure would be true for "blockchain startups" that trade on stock exchanges. There will, without doubt, be future Amazon's and Google's coming out of this cryptocurrency and blockchain boom. However, it's a pretty safe bet that for every one of these future tech giants, there will be at least 5 pets.com type busts.

An additional lesson we can learn from the DOTCOM boom, and one that may well help your own investing, is our tendency as investors to overestimate the speed of adoption of new technology. We've ever seen this as recently as 2 years ago with the 3D printing industry. Hundreds of millions of dollars flooded into the 3D printing space and share prices of 3D printing companies soared. They've since come crashing down, but are still above the level they were 5 years ago.

So don't go heaping all your money into blockchain stocks just yet. There are a number of exciting blockchain projects, and alternative ways to profit from this current market, and I'll be discussing those in greater depth later on in this book.

What everyone needs to know about ICOs

For the uninitiated, Initial Coin Offerings (ICOs) are the process of where a cryptocurrency startup offers its own tokens to the general public, in exchange for funding in the form of other cryptocurrency tokens. The funding tokens are usually Bitcoin or Ethereum, with the vast majority of ICOs being built on Ethereum. However, we are now also seeing ICOs using Neo and Stellar Lumens as a funding source. The exchange rate of BTC or ETH to the new token is pre-determined before the ICO. For example, during gambling platform Funfair's (FUN) ICO used an exchange rate of 1 ETH = 32500 FUN.

For example, in 2014 Ethereum's ICO raised 31,500 Bitcoin with a market value of approximately $18.4 million at the time). Since then we have seen ICOs raise hundreds of millions of dollars worth of Bitcoin or Ethereum. Decentralized storage platform Filecoin currently holds the record for largest ICO at around $257 million.

We have seen ICO investment funds pop up such as Pantera Capital and FinShi Capital. However, due to their relative accessibility, we are seeing more and more consumer investors moving towards ICOs in an attempt to get their slice of the cryptocurrency pie.

Skeptics will say that an ICO is merely a way for a company to raise capital without giving up any equity. This statement has some merit. If you invest in an ICO, you do not own shares of the company, you merely own their token. The token value is tied to company performance for some ICOs, but for others, the tokens may not have any inherent value of their own.

We've seen ICOs revolving around bananas, and a female-centric coin that threatens to "disrupt the patriarchy". We even saw an ICO by the name of "Useless Ethereum Token", whose whitepaper pleaded with people not to invest, raise over $100,000. It goes without saying that as the numbers of ICOs increase, the number of bad ones increases as well. This, combined with a number of ICO whitepapers focusing more on revolutionary language, and large bonuses for early investors to spark a "fear of missing out", has led to some very questionable cryptocurrencies receiving funding. I'm now going to explain a few very basic warning signs that you should look at for before you invest in an ICO.

Fundamental usage of blockchain technologies

Remember how we discussed companies putting "blockchain" in their name then seeing large price increases? We can apply that to ICOs as well. The first major question you should ask yourself is, does this company have an actual need for blockchain technology in their business model?

This goes further, does the token have an actual, or even theoretical use case? The general rule is, the more specific the use case, the better the chances of it being a legitimate operation. If the answer is unclear from the whitepaper, then you should stay well away.

That use case has to go beyond "a store and transfer of value" as well, we already have Bitcoin and then some smaller coins that focus on speed and low transaction fees.

Be careful our promises of token utility within the cryptocurrency's own ecosystem as well. For example, the ability to execute your own smart contracts and pay people via your fingerprint may sound good in theory, but if the ecosystem doesn't exist, then your tokens still have no actual value as of yet.

Percentage of tokens held by founders

Generally speaking, less than 10% of the overall tokens available should go to the founders. There are however ICOs with more than 50% of the tokens reserved for the project founders. ICOs like these are more than likely just a cash grab from a few developers.

Plagiarism in whitepapers

Whitepapers are technical documents outlining how exactly the company's blockchain solution will work, and which industries it will benefit. These documents are lengthy, and often will be over 30 pages long. However, with the rise in ICOs, there is now a rise in less than reputable companies plagiarizing the whitepapers of legitimate ICOs.

There is the case of TRON, which at the time had a market cap of $14 billion, and was accused of copying pages from the Filecoin whitepaper. Founder Justin Sun came out and said the English translation of the whitepaper was done by volunteers who did not understand the scope of the project. TRON has since seen a decline in value of nearly 60% since these allegations were revealed.

The biggest case of this was DADI. The project was called out for plagiarizing large portions of SONM's whitepaper. Significant parts were directly copied and pasted, including citations. It is worrying that a company with a multi-million dollar operation would be careless at worst. The DADI team claims the SONM whitepaper "inspired" them and apologized for the event. I should note that DADI has since revised its whitepaper and now it does not contain any of the same content as SONM's.

Wall Street's Influence on Bitcoin

2017 was the year when Wall Street first starting making big moves into the cryptocurrency space, after dismissing it as merely a fad for so long. This isn't unprecedented by any means, It should be noted that Wall Street is *always* sceptical of new asset classes. We saw it with junk bonds in the 80s, and then internet stocks in the 90s.

In December 2017, a landmark event occurred as Bitcoin futures were launched by the Chicago Mercantile Exchange (CME). This was the first time any cryptocurrency was openly traded on a US regulated trading floor and shortly following the launch we witnessed a 400% increase in Bitcoin prices within less than 6 weeks. Let's make one thing clear, full scale institutional adoption and cryptocurrency trading floors would see colossal price increases in Bitcoin.

What you may not know is that there are now over 100 Bitcoin and blockchain hedge funds in existence, with more new ones starting up every single month.

Early adopters

One area that some early adopters have profited massively is in cryptocurrency arbitrage, the practice of using price disparity on different exchanges to their advantage. This practice is nothing new and has been around in the securities market for centuries, but there are less and less opportunities now with the computerization of everything.

However, cryptocurrency still has massive arbitrage opportunities, with price disparities between exchanges sometimes being as high as 10%. The most notable of these is what is known as the "kimchi premium", as cryptocurrencies on South Korean exchanges tend to trade up to 10, or as much as 15% higher than on US based ones. This phenomenon was so widespread, that the cryptocurrency ticket website coinmarketcap.com had to remove Korean exchanges from their price listings because of said discrepancies.

One such fund taking advantage of this is Virgil Capital, which monitors the price differences on 40 different exchanges around the world. Despite Bitcoin's 28% price drop in January, the fund was up by over 12% after fees. Wall Street's high frequency trading firms such as DRW Holdings are also getting in on the action.

JP Morgan

Jamie Dimon, one of Bitcoin's loudest detractors recently stated he "regrets" calling cryptocurrency a fraud. He also went on to say he believes in blockchain technology. What went unnoticed is that 3 months before this statements, when Dimon was still positioning himself as Mr. Anti-Bitcoin, his own bank launched a blockchain based system. The system aims to lower transaction fees and times for cross-border payments.

The real takeaway from this is that even if Wall Street leaders are openly opposing cryptocurrency, the behind the scenes story is very different indeed. Especially when it comes to implementing blockchain solution that could lead to increased profits for their own business.

Over 60% of Apple shares are held by institutions, others large companies have even higher percentages.

Diversification

Wall Street has taken a liking to cryptocurrencies in recent months because they do not move in line with the stock market. This is known in the finance world as a "non-correlated asset", and represents a great diversification proposition for the customers of these banks. As such, more and more large investment funds are starting to use cryptocurrency as a financial instrument of their own, rather than mocking it as they had done previously.

Diversification in this sense doesn't mean investing in little known altcoins though, institutional money is still attracted to the safer side of things. This is precisely why we saw large increases in both Bitcoin and Ethereum towards the end of 2017.

Correlations between Bitcoin and other cryptocurrencies

As discussed in a previous book, there is a significant correlation between Bitcoin and altcoins. Part of this is a key reason why the small number of investors who are praying for the death of Bitcoin are misguided in their wishes. For now, Bitcoin is still the King of the cryptocurrency space, and the cryptocurrency market as a whole is still very much relying on Bitcoin to continue to grow.

When new money flows into the cryptocurrency market, it always goes into Bitcoin first. This is money both from consumer investors, and institutional ones. This leads to a rise in Bitcoin, but also a dip in altcoin values as money is transferred from altcoins into Bitcoin as holders try to make extra profits.

Conversely, when Bitcoin falls in value - this signals that money is leaving the cryptocurrency space as a whole, and altcoin values decrease as well. This lack of confidence leads to a shrinking of the overall cryptocurrency market cap.

Traditionally, altcoins have performed best when Bitcoin is stable, and not moving significantly in either direction. This is when cryptocurrency investors have sought new opportunities, and what leads them directly to altcoins.

Will Bitcoin eventually be usurped from the top spot by another cryptocurrency? - It's possible. But for now, we should hope that Bitcoin continues to perform well.

One of the big things keeping Bitcoin at the top of the pile is it still maintains its position as the biggest exchange pairing for smaller cryptocurrencies. For those are you who have not yet invested in cryptocurrencies, what this means is that there are only a few cryptocurrencies you can buy directly for fiat currency (like US Dollars or British pounds), for the rest of them you need to buy Bitcoin first, and then exchange Bitcoin into a different cryptocurrency.

However, due to the rise in Bitcoin transaction fees, more and more exchanges are listed Ethereum as the preferred exchange pair. Ethereum possesses faster and lower fee transactions than Bitcoin, and thus at the current time, makes it an ideal exchange pairing. This is one factor that could affect Bitcoin' growth going forward, although it is working on solutions in the form of the upcoming Lightning Network.

Are Bitcoin and Ethereum finally separating?

In the month of January, Bitcoin's market dominance, in other words, Bitcoin's percentage of the total cryptocurrency market cap, halved from 66% to 33%, it's lowest, mark ever and down from a peak of 80% in June 2017.

Traditionally, prices of Ethereum, the number 2 cryptocurrency, have long been tied to Bitcoin's price, and trends have moved in similar directions. However, we are now seeing Ethereum somewhat move towards independence from the incumbent King of Cryptocurrency. There are a number of reasons for this.

In terms of the total number of transactions, Ethereum now accounts for roughly 50% of them, compared to 33% for Bitcoin. At its peak in December 2017, Ethereum was processing over 1 million transactions a day. Then there's the Ethereum ecosystem, 80 out of the top 100 coins on coinmarketcap.com at the time of writing were built on the Ethereum blockchain. The vast majority of ICOs launched in 2017 were Ethereum based ones, and that trend is predicted to continue in 2018 and beyond.

Ethereum trading pairs are now increasing in popularity on major exchanges. Where before users had to use a Bitcoin pairing with another coin, they can now use Ethereum for the same coin. This is preferable to many traders and investors as Ethereum transaction fees are roughly 90% less than those of Bitcoin. In terms of the very largest exchanges, Binance now has 101 out of 103 coins available for trading against Ethereum and BitFinex now accepts all coins traded against Ethereum. This also has ramifications for new entrants to the market, who previously had to buy Bitcoin in order to buy any cryptocurrency. So the new money flowing into the market is now flowing into Ethereum rather than just Bitcoin.

The key ratio to look out for in Ethereum to Bitcoin prices is 0.13, this has traditionally been the level that Ethereum has struggled to break through. If we see a move to even 0.15, this demonstrates that there is inherent confidence in Ethereum as being able to take over the number one spot in the cryptocurrency ecosystem. Due to the higher supply of Ethereum, at the time of writing, a price increase to $1350 would see it overtake Bitcoin and become the number one cryptocurrency in terms of market cap, this is, of course, assuming Bitcoin's price remains stable.

Should you invest in a Bitcoin ETF or Investment Trust?

There are a number of Bitcoin investment trusts and "Bitcoin ETFs" appearing now, on the surface these appear to be a low-risk way to invest in Bitcoin.

One such example of this is the Bitcoin Investment Trust run by Grayscale . The fund owns a fixed amount of Bitcoin on behalf of its investors. In January 2018, the fund decided to perform a 91-for-1 stock split. In other words, for every share owned up to that point would receive an additional 91 shares. Conversely, those shares would be worth 1/91th of the value of the initial share. Under the new pricing structure, each share is worth the equivalent of 0.00101 Bitcoin. The reason for doing this is to lower the base level price and make the fund more accessible to the everyday investor. Share prices fell from $1,970 to a much more consumer friendly $21.65. The aim of this fund is to make owning cryptocurrency as accessible as possible for people.

There are two major problems with this though. Number one, the fund trades at a significant premium when compared to Bitcoin's actual value. A slight premium would be acceptable based on the work involved, however, at current market prices, investors are paying over a 50% premium for Bitcoin under this structure. There's also an additional annual 2% management fee when all the "management" required is holding Bitcoin in a wallet. Taking all this into account, you're better off just buying Bitcoin yourself, with the two easiest methods for a first time investor being Coinbase or Robinhood (if available).

Bitcoin ETFs

There are no pure Bitcoin ETFs available at the time of writing. A public statement by the SEC in January 2018 stated that "significant investor protection issues" needed to be examined before firms could start offering one. There were attempts prior to this to register a Bitcoin ETF, the most notable of which was by the Winklevoss Twins. The twins collectively known as the world's first Bitcoin billionaires after investing much of the money they were paid as part of their successful lawsuit against Facebook's Mark Zuckerberg in Bitcoin back in 2011, had their ETF rejected by the SEC in May 2017.

The solution

There are a number of blockchain ETFs currently available for consumer investors, including the Reality Shares Nasdaq NexGen Economy ETF ($BLCN) and Amplify Transformational Data Sharing ETF (BLOK). Both of these funds track stocks which are either pure blockchain companies or have significant portions of their business dedicated to blockchain.

HLBK

In February 2018, Canadian regulators approved the country's first blockchain based ETF under the ticker HLBK, this ETF is the first North American ETF that actually tracks cryptocurrencies themselves as opposed to just blockchain stocks.

The correlation between Bitcoin and gold

Bitcoin has long been dubbed "digital gold", and Bitcoin billionaire Cameron Winklevoss described at as "gold 2.0" but just how similar are the two assets? Gold, which at the time of writing trades at around $1250 per ounce, has always been "safe haven" asset, the one investors believe will always have intrinsic value, even in the case of a complete stock market collapse. We already discussed how Wall Street has traditionally used gold as a hedge against the stock market and is starting to do the same with cryptocurrencies.

However, that's largely where the similarities end, in fact, it seems that Bitcoin is eating into gold's market share. RJO Futures' Philip Streible stated that "Bitcoin has stolen a large market share of gold". It should be noted that this was before the launch of the Bitcoin futures contract on the CME and CBoE. If Bitcoin took a 5% share of the global gold market, we would be looking at prices of around $50,000 per Bitcoin.

At this point, there is a well documented inversely correlated relationship between Bitcoin and gold. This is when Bitcoin goes up, gold goes down and vice versa. This may well help us predict the future price movements of both assets, as we see in which direction institutional money is moving. A January report

One interesting thing to note in the large downturn of January 2018, was that gold sales rose significantly during the month. On January 16, the first day of the crash, gold sales spiked by a factor of 5. In the same interview s previously quoted, Streibel stated: "If all of a sudden we see Bitcoin futures go into a free fall and collapse, [gold will benefit]."

It should also be noted that silver prices have been in freefall since the rise of Bitcoin and the cryptocurrency market at the beginning of 2017.

9 different expert's Bitcoin price predictions

Everyone loves to predict the future, especially when it could get their name features on a news report on CNBC or Fox. So we're seeing a lot of Bitcoin price predictions for 2018.

For example, a price of $60,000 would see a market cap of $1 trillion. Gold's current market cap is around $9.7 trillion. For reference, the entire cryptocurrency market cap was still below $200 billion in July.

A Monte Carlo simulation, which is based on past investor behaviour run by data scientist Xoel L Barata showed that with an 80% confidence level, the year end price for Bitcoin would be between $13,200 and $271,277. With an equal chance of both possibilities. At the 50th percentile, in other words, the most likely price, the price estimate was around $58,000. According to the simulation, which was run 100,000 times, there is a 9% chance that Bitcoin would end the year at a lower price than it began ($12,951).

Here are a number of other predictions from those on Wall Street and others involved in the cryptocurrency space.

"I wouldn't be surprised if over the next year it's down to $1,000 to $3,000," - Peter Blockvar, CEO, Bleakley Advisory Group

"A lot more money is going to come into Bitcoin, Bitcoin will go up to $30,000-35,000 this year" - Imran Wasim, financial analyst, AMSYS Group

"Even on a risk-adjusted basis, I think bitcoin is going to easily outperform the S&P." "[we can expect] a return to $20,000" - Tom Lee, Fundstrat Global Advisors

"As high as an overvalued $115,000, based on previous behaviour cycles" - Trace Meyer, Blockchain evangelist and early adopter

"Between $50,000 and $100,000 in 2018." - Kay Van Peterson, analyst, Saxo Bank

"all the way down to zero" - Nouriel "Dr. Doom" Roubini, professor of economics, New York University

"[$20,000 based on] An argument can be made that the good news is still not fully reflected in the current price." - Ronnie Moas, founder, Standpoint Research Inc.

"Bitcoin could be $40,000 at the end of this year" - Michael Novogratz, Bitcoin millionaire and Hedge Fund Manager

...plus 1 more from the infamous John McAfee, who promised to eat his own penis on TV if he was incorrect.

"$1 million by 2020"

OK John, we'll see about that one.

The growth of the Internet of Things market

The Internet of Things and blockchain go hand in hand. The IoT industry is estimated to grow around 300% in over the next 5 years and will reach $1.4 trillion by 2021.

Blockchain technology will play a huge part in this. The sheer number of data transactions, between multiple devices on multiple networks, means monitoring all these transactions is incredibly complicated, especially in terms of accountability. Where blockchain comes in is by providing a permanent, transparent and irrefutable record of transfers of both physical goods and data. If there is an error, or something goes wrong, blockchain can see where the error was made, and even rectify said error if possible.

In terms of cryptocurrency, IOTA is the largest one with a strong IoT focus. The coin has already received plaudits as well as investments from major companies such as Bosch. Focusing on just the pharmaceutical sector, Modum (MOD) is one example of the interaction between blockchain and the IoT. This specific use case has massive social benefits in the forms of lowering the circulation of counterfeit drugs and reduce the amount the industry spends on shipping logistics.

IBM is another company that has heavily focused on the IoT and blockchain interactions. The tech giant's biggest move thus far has been to invest over $200 million in it's Watson IoT headquarters, with much of this money going towards integrating blockchain solutions within the company. IBM also recently partnered with shipping giant Maersk to launch a new venture aimed at utilizing blockchain solutions for the shipping industry. Another IBM backed project is Hyperledger, an open source project in collaboration with JP Morgan among other companies that aims to demonstrate to customers how they can use blockchain in their own business.

A smaller company, that may not be on your radar is Filament. The Nevada based blockchain firm produces microchips that can be integrated into products and automatically create their own smart contracts and verify their own transactions. These are all stored on a decentralized server, so there is no risk of tampering. This is a useful alternative to centralized cloud based systems.

The only place where you can trade cryptocurrency and stocks at the same time

Yes, it's true, the development consumer investors have been crying out for is finally here. Stock-trading app Robinhood, known for its zero commission policy, is planning to integrate cryptocurrency trading. This move is sparked by the growing interest in cryptocurrency from younger investors, and those who don't yet have any investments of their own.

After all, 78 percent of Robinhood's customer base is 18-35 year olds, and the app has taken a significant market share in that demographic from traditional leaders like TD Ameritrade. The initial currency pairings will be Bitcoin and Ethereum, both traded against the US Dollar.

This will be the first of its kind, stock trading and cryptocurrency in the same place. It should be noted that this is actual cryptocurrency you are trading, not futures contracts denominated in USD. The initial rollout will be in 5 states (California, Massachusetts, Missouri, New Hampshire and Montana), with purchases limited to below $1,000. Even with these caveats, more than 1 million wannabe investors signed up for the chance to be given early access to the platform. For comparison, the last move of this kind by Robinhood was the announcement of commission free options trading, which garnered just 150,000 sign ups.

It's also worth noting that the new crypto venture will allow users to set price alerts for 14 additional cryptocurrencies. It will be interesting see if these currencies are also adopted by the platform at a later date. Although many of the currencies don't have fiat pairings themselves so that could prove to be troublesome. Robinhood CEO Baiju Bhatt stated that there are future plans to support all of these currencies, which include lesser known ones such as QTUM and Stellar. It remains to be seen if this will be via fiat to crypto pairings or a more traditional model like crypto to crypto pairings. The cryptocurrency move will not include ICOs either, which is in line with Robinhood's current model of not offering OTC stocks within the app.

The interesting development will be seeing if Robinhood can disrupt Coinbase's hold on the consumer cryptocurrency market. Coinbase has revenue of over $1 billion and briefly was the number one downloaded app on the Apple store, yet has its fair share of growing pains. Coinbase has suffered from long support ticket times during the last few months due to the sheer number of new users. Robinhood's initial 5 state rollout plan will be beneficial for them as it will help them test their internal support team's capabilities.

There is also the debate of where Robinhood will store user's coins, and whether investors will be covered in the case of hacks. According to their website, they will be using a mixture of online and offline storage for coins, and have "cutting-edge security measures that are both processes and technologically driven to secure your coins." There are no more specifics than this at the current time, so we will have to wait and see an exact plan for investors going forward.

What will the emergence of the Bitcoin futures market mean for cryptocurrency?

In December 2017, the Chicago Board of Exchange (CBoE) launched the first Bitcoin futures market, the first of its kind in the US. A week later, the Chicago Mercantile Exchange (CME) offered the same contract. This allows traders to buy and sell Bitcoin based on a predicted future price. The initial length of the futures contract was 1 month, with the original asking price being set at $15,000 for 1 Bitcoin. It should be noted that with futures contracts, the Bitcoin tokens themselves do not change hands between traders, and all trades are executed in US dollars only. In the run up to the launch of the CBoE futures, Bitcoin broke $20,000 for the first time based on speculated demand from Wall Street.

Futures contracts being offered have a number of ramifications. The first of which is more liquidity in the market. More money flows in from Wall Street and as more brokers, especially at a consumer level begin to offer their customer this option, could lead to a short term price rise.

There's also the matter of the futures contracts leading to an expanded investor base. Investment banks can now offer futures contracts to their clients as an asset.

The third is overall confidence. The CBoE and CME are both regulated exchanges, which signifies Wall Street's confidence in Bitcoin as a legitimate financial asset. If this confidence spreads to other cryptocurrencies like Ethereum and Ripple, it will only mean good things for the space as a whole.

The long term effects are debatable. If you look at gold as an example, in the first 5 years after gold futures were launched in 1974, there was very little correlation between the futures contracts and the price of gold, which was more influenced by geopolitical events such as the 1979 Soviet invasion of

Afghanistan. The same analysis holds true for silver, which was also largely unaffected int he long term by futures contracts.

Some speculators have debated whether the launch of a futures market for a volatile asset could lead to a 2008 style crash based on bankers not being able to pay their debts. However, this is largely based on questionable "what-if" scenarios than anything to do with cryptocurrencies themselves.

It should also be noted that initial uptake of futures contracts on the CBoE was slow compared to other futures markets like gold or forex. On the first day of trading there were approximately 3,500 trades made compared to 400,000 daily for the gold futures market.

What every potential investor needs to know about Ripple (XRP)

Cryptocurrency investors have long been aware of Ripple, the payment platform that focuses on partnerships with large, already established, financial institutions. Ripple and its token XRP entered the mainstream media in December 2017 after a meteoric rise saw the coin's value soar from $0.25 to a peak of more than $3. If we look at the year as a whole, Ripple was the highest returning cryptocurrency with gains of over 37,000%, making creator Chris Larson one of the world's richest men based on his XRP holdings.

Today Ripple can boast of partnerships with mega banks like Santander, credit card provider American Express and international transfer service MoneyGram. The later is perhaps the most important, as it saves MoneyGram users huge amounts in transaction fees.

How does Ripple work? Simply put, transfers are made from one currency (like the US dollar) into XRP (Ripple's token), then the XRP is converted into a second currency (like Yen). The base level transaction cost for this is just 0.00001 XRP which is just a fraction of a cent, and much lower than traditional cross border payment systems like SWIFT.

This all sounds extremely promising, and Ripple is probably the most well developed cryptocurrency outside of Bitcoin and Ethereum, In terms of real world adoption and partnerships. However, there are a number of things to note about holding Ripple.

Ripple vs. XRP

By buying XRP, you are not buying shares in Ripple Labs. The major underlying point here is that XRP is not required for the Ripple network to function (other currencies can be used), nor are banks required to use XRP in order to partner up with Ripple. It should be noted therefore that banks do not directly buy XRP like they do with Bitcoin. There is no large scale institutional level investment in XRP.

Where the confusion lies is that if a private investor invests in Ripple company, the incorrect assumption is made that the value of XRP should also increase. However, XRP token's valuation and Ripple company's financial situation are irrelevant.

Competition

Ripple currently has the capability to process around 1,500 transactions per second which is roughly 200 times that of the Bitcoin network. However, there are other cryptocurrencies emerging that are potentially even faster. RaiBlocks (XRB) for example has processed over 7,000 transactions per second on its test network, and a little known cryptocurrency XtraBytes (XBY) has outlined the steps needed to process over 10,000 transactions per second.

XRP Supply issues

A third thing to note about XRP, is that only 40% of the tokens are currently in circulation. A further 20% of the tokens are held by the founders themselves. Ripple Labs controls the supply of XRP issued, so unlike a decentralized approach like that of Bitcoin or Ethereum, they can release XRP as they wish. This means they could release large amounts of XRP to the market, which would lead to significant inflation and a decrease in value of the current XRP token. It should be noted that you cannot mine XRP, and must rely on Ripple Labs for the supply of the token.

Banks creating their own solution

Due to Ripple's targeting of large financial institutions, this leaves them vulnerable to competition from the banks themselves. Many banks including Barclays and HSBC are working to develop their own blockchain solution for cross border payments. One area banks have to their advantage is that it is much easier to sell a blockchain solution internally to upper management than it is for an outside company to pitch one. In terms of development speed, this is another area where banks have an advantage as they have much deeper pockets than Ripple Labs.

An analysis of Blockchain based stocks and stocks which utilize blockchain technology

If cryptocurrencies are still overwhelming, confusing or too risky for you - that's OK.

You can still very much profit from blockchain technology in the regular stock market. Below are some companies that are utilizing blockchain technology in their own unique way.

Once again, I should note that I am not recommending or advising you buy any of the stocks listed here.

Alphabet Inc. ($GOOG)

Price at time of writing: $1,175.58

We start with one you've probably all heard of, unless you've not only been living under a rock but an entire mountain! Google is actually the second largest blockchain investor over the past 5 years through its investment arm, Google Ventures.

One of their most recent investments was that of Storj (discussed in depth in one of my previous books - *Ethereum: Beginners Bible).* Storj offers consumer and enterprise level blockchain solutions for decentralized online storage. Storj will act as a competitor to traditional cloud solutions like Amazon Web Services and AliBaba's Cloud service. Other notable investments from Google Ventures include cross-border payment processor Veem.

Overstock ($OSTK)

Price at time of writing: $86.90

Overstock.com is a fairly under the radar boomer from the past few months. Like the company's name suggests, they deal in excess manufactured goods and sell them at a deep discount. This is everything from furniture, to sporting goods to jewelry - but nothing revolutionary right?

However, Overstock was the first major retailer to accept Bitcoin as a payment method, way back in 2014, which sparked the first wave of cryptocurrency adoption on main street. The company also owns a subsidiary called Medici Ventures, which is focused solely on investing in, and developing blockchain technology. Medici holdings has invested heavily in a number of blockchain products, most notably the cryptocurrency Factom. Investments like have seen Overstock's price rise over 400% in less than 6 months. More importantly, these are exactly the kinds of patterns we want to look out for when examining how we use blockchain technology to profit from traditional stocks.

SBI Holdings (NASDAQ:SBHGF)

Price at time of writing: $25.30

Based out of Japan, but also listed on the NASDAQ, SBI Holdings which is part of the SBI Group. The firm gained notoriety after investing heavily in the Japanese Bitcoin exchange BitFlyer and in a move that garnered more mainstream attention, the cryptocurrency Ripple. SBIs investment in Ripple included using the platform to test cross-border payments between Japan and South Korea. The investment in Ripple was one of the key catalysts that not only saw Ripple's price increase, but also those that adopted its technology.

SBI continued their cryptocurrency charge in October by making a move into mining. The company released a statement outlining the motivations for their move saying.

"The SBI Group will endeavor to acquire cryptocurrencies, for the further development of products and services, and to secure market liquidity. This includes the mining of [bitcoin and bitcoin cash], and investments into U.S. Ripple"

IBM ($IBM)

Price at time of writing: $166.80

It should come as no surprise that a company that's always been on the forefront of the tech industry is betting on blockchain. In October the tech giant announced a partnership with then little known cryptocurrency Stellar, aimed at utilizing Stellar's payment platform for banking focused on 12 countries in the South Pacific region, including Australia and New Zealnd. IBM has a huge overseas customer base and thus is always looking for ways to save money on cross-border transfers.

This seal of approval if you will from the financial sector, leads us to the next step in blockchain technology, going from strictly theoretical, to being used mainly in cryptocurrency, to the next step which represents true widespread adoption.

This caused not only a positive bump in IBM stock but also a whopping 127% overnight growth in the price of Stellar Lumens (XLM) itself. This goes to show that adoption works both ways. Traditional companies benefit from blockchain solutions, and the cryptocurrencies themselves benefit from adoption by these companies. It's pretty safe to say that going into 2018 and beyond, we'll only be seeing more of these types of partnerships.

Mining based stocks - An often overlooked opportunity

Two of the biggest cryptocurrency winners in the past few years, haven't been cryptocurrencies themselves, but ones that are affected by the boom in cryptocurrency mining.

You see, mining cryptocurrency requires a huge amount of computing power, in the form of Central Processing Units (CPUs) and Graphics Processing Units (GPUs). Manufacturers of these parts have seen their stock prices skyrocket since the beginning of 2016 when cryptocurrency mining really took off.

AMD ($AMD) and NVIDIA ($NVDA) are the two biggest winners thus far, in fact, in Q3 2017, NVIDIA's revenue from mining soared to $220 million for the quarter. Now, nearly 5% of the company's bottom line is attributable to cryptocurrency mining. AMD, on the other hand, sees roughly 10% of its overall revenue being from cryptocurrency mining sources.

So is it time to go long on AMD & NVDA - not so fast. There are a number of factors at play which will have a large effect on prices.

What if mining decreases in popularity?

It could be argued that due to the nature of cryptocurrencies, miner payouts will continue to decrease (like in the case of Bitcoin and Ethereum). There have also been suggestions that as cryptocurrencies develop, there may not be a need for GPU mining at all.

There's also the wildcard of Ethereum switching to Proof of Stake mining which will make GPU mining for Ethereum obsolete. This switch was originally scheduled for 2017 but was delayed at least a year, and there are rumors swirling that the switch may not happen before 2019 now. For the time being though, miners are currently earning around $1.76 profit per GPU per day from mining Ethereum, which may seem low on the surface, but you have mining farms with thousands of GPUs, these profits add up fast.

Either way, the companies themselves have different approaches to how cryptocurrencies will affect their profits going forward. AMD CEO Lisa Su stated that they were expecting a "cryptocurrency cooling off period" in 2018, and the company doesn't consider demand for GPUs as a part of its long term gameplan.

NVIDIA, on the other hand, is more bullish and has openly admitted that it considers cryptocurrency mining a big part of future business plans.

What if China bans mining?

70% of the world's cryptocurrency mining operations are in China, however, China is volatile when it comes to cryptocurrency, to say the least. We've already seen the government ban Chinese citizens from investing in ICOs outside of China, which had a significant detrimental effect on the market. So naturally, there is some concern that a mining ban or cutback or any kind could immediately send any mining based stock into free fall.

However, Bitmain Technologies, the owner of one of the world's largest mining operations is looking to expand it's operations to Canada and Switzerland to mitigate some of this risk. Canada is on its radar due to the generous tax incentives offered by Manitoba and Saskatchewan provinces.

Additional mining resources

There are two more ETFs that specialize in semiconductor companies that make the computer chips required for mining. These being the iShares PHLX Semiconductor ETF (SOXX) and VanEck Vectors Semiconductor ETF (SMH). Both of these funds have seen significant growth as a result of the mining movement, and their future success will be heavily determined by the continued uptake of cryptocurrency mining.

Will Central Banks issue cryptocurrencies of their own?

This is a central (pardon the pun) question that we should all be asking going forward. Will central banks launch their own cryptocurrencies in 2018? This question a tricky one for financial, technological and ideological reasons.

We'll address the ideological reason first as they are the most simple. Part of the identity of cryptocurrency as a whole comes from being a solution to centralized institutions having control of our money.

What we need to note though is one extremely important distinction. Central banks have significantly different financial goals from the consumer investor. The consumer investor wants to maximize their returns in the shortest possible time, and with cryptocurrencies, we've seen this more than ever. Central banks on the other have an obligation to provide financial stability for the citizens of that particular country.

It's for this reason that we're unlikely to see central banks holding large amounts of any cryptocurrency, whose volatility makes it a less than ideal asset in their eyes. However, banks still want to embrace blockchain technology, which leads us to the natural solution to this, central banks launching their own cryptocurrencies.

These currencies would be available for the citizens of each country to buy, but unlike regular cryptocurrencies these would likely be pegged to that country's base currency. The question is however, is they are pegged to the base currency, what incentive is there for consumers to hold a central bank owned cryptocurrency? It takes away the consumer's main motivation of short-term profits because it functions the same as holding your money in a bank account, except on a blockchain. You could argue that holding any money on a blockchain is more secure than storing it with a private bank. However in first world countries, bank deposits are all automatically insured up to a certain amount anyway, so in practical terms, the two would function the same.

So the second way in which banks could use their own cryptocurrencies is in a way similar to Ripple, as an intermediary payment processor. The question there, is if they could reasonably develop a system better than a privately owned on (like XRP) or decentralized cryptocurrency (like XRB). This is likely to be low down on a bank's list of priorities, so it's unlikely that we'll be seeing a central bank cryptocurrency in the near future. That doesn't mean they won't be looking to profit from blockchain technology, so it'd be wise to monitor blockchain solutions for partnerships with central banks.

The next best alternative to a cryptocurrency ETF

For those of you familiar with traditional investments, then you'll likely to be aware of Exchange Traded Funds or ETFs. For those unfamiliar, an ETF is a security that trades like a regular stock, but instead of buying shares in one company, you are buying an aggregate of many companies. ETFs have an inherent advantage over single stocks in that by diversifying your risk over many companies, you are less likely to see sudden drops in price.

Based out of Slovenia, and active since November 2016, Fintech start-up Iconomi is currently running a blockchain based digital asset management platform using Ethereum technology. Known as Digital Asset Arrays (DAA), these are similar to ETFs and Index funds, as you are buying an aggregate of multiple cryptocurrencies instead of just one or two. Initial investments can be made with ETH or BTC, although there are plans to support fiat deposits in the coming months.

Their BLX blockchain index is the first passively managed array of digital assets, compromising of over 20 different cryptocurrencies, with the highest weight being in Bitcoin and Ethereum. The portfolio is re-balanced on a monthly basis, and different cryptocurrencies are added and removed based on performance. What's more is the BLX has currently outperformed both Ethereum and Litecoin over the past 6 months. There is also a more conservative fund which is composed of 60% Bitcoin, 20% Ethereum as well as 4 other ERC20 tokens. All Iconomi funds have a 2-3% annual management fee, plus a 0.5% exit fee.

This could well be a good option if you're looking to invest in a multitude of cryptocurrencies, but don't want to deal with the hassle of signing up for multiple exchanges, and keeping track of various wallets. Iconomi currently offers 15 different DAAs, ranging from conservative, heavily Bitcoin based ones, to more risky ones featuring a multitude of smaller cap cryptocurrencies. Of course, like any investment, there are inherent risks involved, but if you're a more risk averse investor, who still wants to be a part of the cryptocurrency market, Iconomi is worth checking out.

How to buy your first cryptocurrency - even if you're a technophobe

Gone are the days when buying Bitcoin was a time consuming and somewhat uncomfortable endeavor. Nowadays buying Bitcoin is a similar process to exchanging currency when you go on vacation. While I previously discussed Robinhood as an option, until the nationwide rollout occurs, and limits are increased, Coinbase still represents the best option for the majority of people.

There are two ways to buy Bitcoin, the first is to use fiat currency (USD, EUR, GBP etc.) to purchase cryptocurrency via an exchange. These exchanges function the same way as regular foreign currency exchanges do. The prices fluctuate on a daily basis, and like regular currency exchange markets - they are open 24/7. These exchanges make their money from charging a small fee for each transaction.

Some charge both buyers and sellers, some only charge a fee for buying. For security reasons, most of these exchanges will require you to verify your ID before allowing you to purchase cryptocurrency.

It is also important to note the type of payments each exchange supports. Some allow for debit/credit card payments whereas other only accept PayPal or bank wire transfers. Below are the three biggest and reputable currency exchanges for purchasing Bitcoin, Ethereum and other altcoins with fiat currency like US dollars, Euros or British Pounds.

Coinbase

Currently largest currency exchange in the world, Coinbase allows users to buy, sell and store cryptocurrency. Coinbase is undoubtedly the most beginner friendly exchange for anyone looking to get involved in the cryptocurrency market. They currently allow trading of Bitcoin, as well as, Ethereum and LiteCoin using fiat currency as a base. Known for their stellar security procedures and insurance policies regarding stored currency. The exchange also has a fully functioning iPhone and Android app for buying and selling on the go, very useful if you are looking to trade.

Once you are signed up and complete the identity verification procedures you can buy Bitcoin with your credit or debit card instantly.

Coinbase also recently launched the Coinbase Vault, which is a secure way of storing your cryptocurrency while still having it accessible to trade. The vault uses double email address + phone verification in order to access your funds. If you're planning on holding long-term, I still recommend offline storage - but as an intermediary option, the Vault is a step in the right direction.

If you sign up for Coinbase using this link, you will receive $10 worth of free Bitcoin after your first purchase of more than $100 worth of cryptocurrency.

http://bit.ly/10dollarbtc

Note, if you're going to be trading Bitcoin, I recommend doing so on Coinbase's partner platform GDax, which has lower fees.

Where to buy altcoins?

Binance and Bittrex are the two largest altcoins trading platform, and both of these now feature Ethereum as well as Bitcoin pairings for nearly all of the coins available. It's on platforms like these where you can purchase popular altcoins such as Neo (NEO), Cardano (ADA), VeChain (VEN) and Stellar Lumens (XLM). Personally I prefer the Binance interface more, but in reality, the two sites are very similar in function.

I should note that I no longer recommend Bitfinex after they stopped serving US customers completely in November 2017. Customers from other countries can still use Bitfinex and it is a perfectly fine platform for those outside the United States. Apart from these, Cryptopia is another good exchange for a number of smaller cap cryptocurrencies such as Bytom and Xtrabytes. Liqui.io also comes recommended as does EtherDelta. All recommendations are based on my personal experience with the platforms and I do not recommend any platforms that I haven't personally used.

Conclusion

So there we have it, a look into how Wall Street and some of the world's top financial institutions are playing this cryptocurrency mania we've been seeing of the past 12 months.

We've covered both the cryptocurrencies themselves, and also how this market affects traditional securities, as well as gold. Hopefully this has given you a greater understanding of the relationships between these 3, and some additional knowledge that you can apply to your own investment strategies.

Just how cryptocurrency will play out in 2018, not even the best and brightest minds in the financial world could tell us, but one thing is for certain, it's going to be a wild ride either way. We need to take a step back and think about the potential applications of blockchain technology beyond just finance, and appreciate just how exciting this technology is. It's rare that we see truly life changing advancements in fields like financial monitoring, supply chain management and even healthcare, but blockchain has the ability to provide all of these.

I encourage you to do your own research on top of what you have read in this book and to not rely on one single source for your cryptocurrency news. If you would like to do some further reading, in my opinion the two best resources for unbiased news on cryptocurrency and blockchain developments are coindesk.com and cointelegraph.com.

As with any investment, never invest more than you can afford to lose. This is a volatile market the likes of which we have never seen before, and as such should be looked at as a high risk investment. For those over the age of 30, I recommend cryptocurrency be no more than 15% of your overall portfolio holdings. For those under 30, this can be increased to 25% due to your greater future earning potential.

I wish you the best of luck in your own cryptocurrency journey, and if you are invested, or decide to invest in the future, I hope you make a lot of money.

Thanks for reading,

Stephen

P.S. Don't forget - if you're a cryptocurrency first timer, you can get $10 worth of Bitcoin for free after spending $100 or more on any cryptocurrency at Coinbase using this link http://bit.ly/10dollarbtc

Cryptocurrency: 13 More Coins to Watch with 10X Growth Potential in 2018

By Stephen Satoshi

Introduction - Cryptocurrency as we head into 2018

2017 was undoubtedly the year that Cryptocurrency arrived on the world stage. The total market cap surged from $18 billion on January 1st to over $600 billion by the end of the year. Coinbase became the world's number one most downloaded app and saw transaction volume increase by a factor of 30.

Bitcoin hit $20,000 per coin very briefly in December. Ethereum went from $9 to over $700, and Litecoin finally broke out and hit $300 by the end of the year. Average returns for investing over the 12 month period range from 200% on the low end, to over 1000%. Frankly, if you put money into cryptocurrency in 2017, it was near impossible to lose.

One of the most startling statistics of 2017 was that if you had invested $100 into the top 10 market cap coins on January 1st, you would have seen returns of $43,000 over the course of the year.

But how does that affect us going forward? Will we have a repeat of last year and see gigantic market growth once more? We'd all sure like to hope so. It's likely though that the market will be a little more nuanced as we progress.

It's clear now that cryptocurrency isn't just "internet gimmick money", we are truly witnessing the birth of a brand new asset class. Institutional money is flowing into the market just as fast as consumer money. There are multiple cryptocurrency ETFs in the works and December saw the launch of Bitcoin futures on CME, the world's largest futures exchange.

But to those of us who are in search of projects with potential for huge growth, 10X, 100X or even 1000X growth, that we now know is completely possible within the cryptocurrency space, we have to dig a little deeper. That's why in this book I'm listing 13 coins with huge possibilities in 2018. Coins with exciting ideas, projects and use cases. Some of them may be more familiar to you than others, but every single one of them has been hand picked based on my own criteria, and you can rest assured that many other coins were discarded in the selection process.

I wish you the very best in your cryptocurrency investing journey, and I hope you make a lot of money.

Thanks,

Stephen

Factors that affect coin growth

Continued Adoption

It's easy to forget sometimes that we are still very much in the early stages of the market. Cryptocurrency may have quickly reached a $600 billion market cap, but that is still dwarfed by the $200 trillion market cap of stocks, cash, gold and bonds combined. And blockchain technology as a whole still has a huge amount of growing to do.

Adoption of coins both as payment methods for currency based coins, as well as, partnerships with larger corporations for non-currency based ones will lead to continued growth going forward.

Coinbase

Coinbase, the cryptocurrency exchange app ended 2017 having hit the number one download spot on the Apple store and Google Play store. The vast majority of the new players into the market (and that may well include yourself), got their start with Coinbase. The convenience of being able to buy and sell cryptocurrency on the go using a credit card is something that favors mass adoption. Especially when compared to previous years when complex wire transfer processes made cryptocurrency much harder for the average person to buy.

As you may know, however, Coinbase currently only deals with 3 cryptocurrencies. Namely, Bitcoin, Ethereum and Litecoin. However, Coinbase Co-Founder and CEO Asiff Hiriji stated in December 2017 that the platform plans to add more coins in the coming months. With rumors about which coins would be added driving up the price of a number of altcoins including Ripple and Bitcoin Cash.

Needless to say, the next coin to be added on Coinbase will see short term positive effects regardless of its long term potential. Much of the cryptocurrency buying public won't be able to wait to get their hands on the shiniest new coin. However, exactly which coins would be added is still largely unknown, although we can make some educated guesses into which ones *won't* be next in line.

Monero - Its status as a complete privacy coin conflicts with Coinbase's position as an SEC regulated entity and their anti-money laundering provisions. The same applies to coins like **ZCash.**

Neo - NEO is not divisible like other cryptocurrencies, and could technically be classified as a security which pays a dividend (in the form of GAS). This makes it hard for Coinbase to add it due to being bound by SEC regulations.

It should also be noted that there are multiple fake images online showing Dash, Monero and Ripple added to Coinbase. Please check the official website before buying or selling on other exchanges based on news of Coinbase additions.

Update: As of December 20th 2017, Bitcoin Cash was added to Coinbase

Bitcoin

Like it or not, Bitcoin's price still carries a lot of the new money being flooded into the market. Although this may prove to be less of an issue going forward as many first time buyers are now investing in Ethereum or Litecoin as their first venture into the cryptocurrency market, Bitcoin is still a major factor in determining overall market sentiment.

The cryptocurrency flowchart generally goes like this.

1. New investors buy Bitcoin with fiat currency as their first foray into the market > Bitcoin's price goes up

2. As Bitcoin's price goes up, altcoin holders move their money into Bitcoin > Altcoin prices go down

3. If Bitcoin's price falls, those holding Bitcoin cash out to fiat, signaling decreased market confidence > Bitcoin & altcoin prices go down

4. If Bitcoin's price remains stable, investors begin to look for new opportunities and begin researching and buying altcoins > altcoin prices rise

If you track the BTC vs. Altcoin patterns in 2017, this generally holds true. Altcoins perform best when Bitcoin prices are stable, and not moving much in either direction. Large movements in Bitcoin price generally have negative effect on altcoin prices.

Legislation

Cryptocurrency leglisation is still a hot topic, and one where we are still largely in the unknown. Poorly researched news articles with headlines such as "Chinese government bans Bitcoin" tend to be the ones that are the most read, even if their factual accuracy is debatable at best.

Cryptocurrency at its core ideals has always been a decentralized idea. In other words, the entire existence is predicated on moving away from control by a single central government. However, in practical terms, especially where investments and securities are concerned, there does have to be some form of recognition by governments, at a national level at least.

For US citizens, the number one short term concern would be senate bill including digital currencies as part of current anti-money laundering laws. These laws would force traders to reveal indentities in certain circumstances, which would obviously hamper the growth of privacy based cryptocurrencies such as Monero, ZCash and Verge. This is also a concern for both UK and EU citizens, whose governments are working on their own version of similar rulings.

Asian legislation is another area of concern, with China and South Korea being under the spotlight specifically. These two markets represent the largest portion of the cryptocurrency space, and government clampdowns from both of these countries have had negative effects on the overall market as recently as mid 2017.

Atomic Swaps

Atomic swaps are one of the most fascinating cryptocurrency developments as we move into 2018, and one that is sure to affect many coins going forward. Atomic swaps allow coin conversions, without the need for a third party. For example, if you own 1 Bitcoin and your friend owns 100 Litecoin, and you want to swap. Currently you would have to use a third party exchange to do so. Third party exchanges require both fees and a degree of trust.

However, by using atomic swaps, there is no need for a third party as both the sender and recipient could confirm the transaction themselves by using what is known as a hash-time limited contract (HTLC). An HTLC is essentially a one-time code that would be generated as part of the swap, that is required to verify its success. If the code is not entered by either party, the transaction will be reversed and both parties will receive their initial coins back.

Up to this point, we have only seen atomic swaps used in very limited amounts, because cryptocurrencies are running on different blockchains, and we need them to share the same cryptographic hash function. The implementation of Lightning Network would allow this to occur. Currently, successful atomic swaps have been carried out between Litecoin, Bitcoin, Vertcoin and a few other coins. Coins that are capable of atomic swaps may well have significant first mover advantage going forward.

Coin Prices & Fractions

I know what you're thinking, I bought this book just to be told the price of a coin matters?! First, let me expand on this rather obvious statement. Cryptocurrencies are unique in the sense that many of them (with notable exceptions like Neo) are divisible into tiny fractions. Bitcoin, for example, is available down to 8 decimal digits, so you could go on an exchange and buy 0.0000001 Bitcoin.

Why does this matter? Simply put, it's extremely confusing to new investors who have previously only bought entire shares of companies. Therefore, they would rather buy 1 of a certain cryptocurrency, than a fraction of another - especially if there are no other deciding factors between the two. It appears easier to buy a "whole" of one coin versus a fraction of another. Therefore, coins with a low $ price are inherently more attractive, even if they have a huge market cap and have less room for potential growth than coins with a lower supply and market cap, but a high $ price per coin.

For example, Ripple currently trades at around $0.50 per XRP, and is seen as "cheap" by many inexperienced buyers, despite its huge market cap. The same applies to Stellar Lumens which trades at around $0.28 per XLM.

Factors to Consider Before Investing

While larger cryptocurrencies like Bitcoin, Ethereum and Litecoin have long track records and multiple real world functions, some of the coins mentioned in this book do not - hence their lower price.

There are a number of different variables to investigate before you undertake any investment, and cryptocurrency has its own set.

Proof of Concept (PoC)

In other words, does the technology have a working model, or is it still in a theoretical stage. Obviously more mature coins will have a higher value, with the more theoretical coins being a bigger risk. As the different coins here are in different stages of their life cycle, that is up for you to decide.

The Development Team

Who are the developers and what is their track record? Particularly within the cryptocurrency and blockchain space. Another thing to consider their record within the particular industry they are targeting, and if they have industry connections are not.

The Utility Of The Coin

Ideas are great, but if the coin token itself doesn't have usage, then the true potential of the project must be questioned. This is especially true in the case of certain coins where the theory and market potential checks out, but the question of "why can I just use Bitcoin/Litecoin to do the same thing" is often raised.

The Roadmap

Roadmaps are important for short-term gains because they set out development targets for the coin. If these goals are reached and the products/platforms move from alpha to beta to a fully launched product, then that only means positive things for the coin and its value. However continually missed targets are a red flag.

Which exchanges is the coin listed on

Many of these coins are still only available on smaller exchanges. Once the coin is listed on larger exchanges, with Coinbase being the biggest and most accessible, the coin has greater visibility and this leads to a rise in value.

Mining Algorithm - Proof of Work vs. Proof of Stake vs. Proof of Signature

You'll notice later on when discussing individual coins that I talk about which mining algorithms are used. The two most popular are Proof of Work (PoW), used by Bitcoin and Proof of Stake (PoS), which will be used by Ethereum from Q4 2017 and beyond, and is currently used by a number of Ethereum based tokens. There is also Proof of Signature (PoSIGN), which is used by newer projects including Xtrabytes.

How to Buy Bitcoin, Ethereum or Litecoin

Gone are the days when buying cryptocurrency was a time consuming and somewhat uncomfortable endeavor. Nowadays buying Bitcoin and other popular cryptocurrencies is a similar process to exchanging currency when you go on vacation.

If you haven't purchased any cryptocurrency before, what you need to do first is to use fiat currency (USD, EUR, GBP etc.) to purchase cryptocurrency via an exchange. These exchanges function the same way as regular foreign currency exchanges do. The prices fluctuate on a daily basis, and like regular currency exchange markets - they are open 24/7. Exchanges make their money by charging a small fee for each transaction.

Some charge both buyers and sellers, some only charge a fee for buying. For security reasons, most of these exchanges will require you to verify your ID before allowing you to purchase cryptocurrency.

It is also important to note the type of payments each exchange supports. Some allow for debit/credit card payments whereas other only accept PayPal or bank wire transfers.

Coinbase

Currently largest currency exchange in the world, Coinbase allows users to buy, sell and store cryptocurrency. Coinbase is undoubtedly the most beginner friendly exchange for anyone looking to get involved in the cryptocurrency market. They currently allow trading of Bitcoin, as well as, Ethereum and LiteCoin using fiat currency as a base. Known for their stellar security procedures and insurance policies regarding stored currency. The exchange also has a fully functioning iPhone and Android app for buying and selling on the go, very useful if you are looking to trade.

Once you are signed up and complete the identity verification procedures you can buy Bitcoin with your credit or debit card instantly.

Coinbase also recently launched the Coinbase Vault, which is a secure way of storing your cryptocurrency while still having it accessible to trade. The vault uses double email address + phone verification in order to access your funds. If you're planning on holding long-term, I still recommend offline storage - but as an intermediary option, the Vault is a step in the right direction.

If you sign up for Coinbase using this link, you will receive $10 worth of free Bitcoin after your first purchase of more than $100 worth of cryptocurrency.

http://bit.ly/10dollarbtc

Note: As of 12/20/17 - Coinbase now also allows users to buy and sell Bitcoin Cash

How do I buy these altcoins if I can not buy them in my local currency?

Buying altcoins can be confusing at first because the vast majority of them aren't available to buy in exchange for fiat currency. Therefore, there are a few steps to go through, but not to worry, because here is a step by step guide to buy altcoins.

1. **Create an account on Coinbase**

Coinbase is still the easiest way for most people to get involved in the cryptocurrency market. Once you sign up (remember to use the link http://bit.ly/10dollarbtc to get $10 worth of Bitcoin for free after your first transaction)

2. **Buy Bitcoin, Ethereum or Litecoin**

You can either do this directly on Coinbase, or by transferring your money to Coinbase's sister site GDax which has lower transaction fees. You can use your Coinbase login credentials to access GDax.

Once you have bought your coins, they will be automatically transferred to your wallet on the respective site. Remember, if you are buying purely for the sake of exchanging coins for the altcoins mentioned in this book, then I recommend buying ETH rather than BTC because the transfer fees will be much lower.

3. **Send coins to your exchange of choice**

I have listed which exchanges to buy these coins at, on the individual coin page under "where to buy". Create an account on that particular website and go to the "deposit" page. Once on the page select your respective coin's wallet (double check you haven't selected the wrong one), and generate an address

You address will be a string of alphanumeric characters similar to this

0x0ded6e1e425eeb3876269c6ae93df77944acf4eee4fe1d7ccd77b185dce1d207

Go to the send coins page on your Coinbase/GDax account and copy the above address into the "recipient" box, and click confirm. This will show your transaction fee as well (for ETH it is currently around $0.40 per transaction).

4. **Use your coins to exchange for altcoins**

Once the transaction has gone through and your coins are now showing up in your new wallet, you can exchange them for the altcoins of your choice. For example, if you want to buy XLM, you can select the XLM/ETH pairing on the exchange.

How to save up to $20 on each altcoin transaction

One of the major problems we face right now in cryptocurrency is the sheer strain on the network as it tries to keep up with increased demand. Transaction fees and transaction times have been dramatically increasing since Mid-November, and new investors are realizing the hard way when they try to transfer their coins from where they bought them, to another exchange.

Many websites give instructions of "Buy bitcoin first, then send to an exchange". However, this is fundamentally wrong and will cost you money. It is much cheaper to buy and send Ethereum for the purpose of exchanging it with one of the coins listed below. The same applies to Litecoin, but there are much fewer Litecoin/altcoin pairs available when compared to Bitcoin and Ethereum.

Currently the approximate transaction prices for each coin are as follows

Bitcoin: $17

Ethereum: $0.40

Litecoin: $0.13

Coins to Watch in 2018

WaBi (WABI)

Price at Time of Writing: $2.00

Market Cap at Time of Writing: $90,339,960

Available on:

BTC: Binance

ETH: Binance, EtherDelta

Where to store:

WaBi can be stored on MyEtherWallet or the Mist desktop wallet

WaBi is a Chinese based blockchain initiative that focuses on anti-counterfeiting for physical products. Born out of the 2012 Chinese milk scandal, that saw 6 children die and over 50,000 hospitalized as a result of fake baby milk formula, the project aims to battle the $500 billion counterfeiting industry.

WaBi's solution to this is linking products using RFID labels with a built-in anti-counterfeit measure. Using Walimai's anti-counterfeiting RFID technology allows consumers to verify the authenticity of the product using their smartphone. Blockchain technology comes into this by verifying product authenticity on a decentralized digital ledger that would allow anyone to see which products are authentic and which ones are not. This essentially creates a secure link between the digital and physical domains. This has ramifications for so many consumer goods industries including baby food, pharmaceuticals, alcohol, clothing and electronics.

This bold venture faces many challenges, especially as there are physical products involved, which in itself has its own set of hurdles. For example, deterioration of product labels, can the labels be securely attached for the entirety of the product's lifespan, and if not, can they be replaced with counterfeit labels?

However, after 3 years of development, the WaBi team has now successfully created a working product as of December 2016, and their tags feature both a unique encrypted product ID and geolocation data of the product source I.e. which factory it was manufactured at. So counterfeiters would have to be able to replicate both of these if they wanted to produce a fake version of the same product, which would prove near impossible unless they have access to the exact same factory where the authentic version of the product is produced.

There is also the issue of consumer trust, can consumers really be sure that the authenticity data is accurate? Well, that's where blockchain technology comes in. Because records are publicly available, and constantly updated in real time, there is no inherent reason not to trust them.

The next level of this trust is the facilitation of consumer to consumer or peer to peer sales. The problem with traditional peer to peer platforms like eBay, and newer ones such as social media based selling, has always been the prevalence of counterfeit goods. As this selling platforms are not under the same legal scrutiny as traditional ones, sellers of counterfeit goods often get away with it. By utilizing WaBi technology, a potential buyer can verify the authenticity of any product *before* the sale goes through, which ensures that all transaction and products are legitimate. The platform has already undergone testing in China, both in ecommerce and in physical stores.

The WaBi token itself will be given to customers every time they scan an item. There are plans for these token to then be used as a loyalty incentive for customers to purchase products with the token as opposed to cash.

2018 will see WaBi roll out to over 1,000 stores across China. Price action in the short term will largely dependent on the token being available on more exchanges because Binance alone is not enough to support increased token demand.

Neo (NEO)

Price at Time of Writing - $72.25

Market Cap at Time of Writing - $4,696,120,000

Available on:

Fiat: Yunbi (CN), Jubi (CN), Livecoin

BTC: Bittrex, Binance, Bitfinex

ETH: Bittrex

Where to store:

Wallets are available on the official Neo website

I previously discussed Neo in my first book *Cryptocurrency: Beginners Bible.* Since then the price has risen by over 900%, and a number of exciting new developments have occurred with the Neo project, so I thought an update would be appropriate as we move into 2018.

One of these earliest Chinese based blockchain projects, Neo, formerly known as Antshares, prides itself on being open source and community driven. The coin has been compared to Ethereum in the sense that it runs smart contracts instead of acting as a simple token like Bitcoin. The project is developed by a Shanghai based company called ONCHAIN.

In a June 2017 press conference held at the Microsoft China HQ in Beijing, the Antshares founder Da Hongfei announced the rebranding to Neo as well as discussing other projects in the pipeline. These included collaborating with certificate authorities in China to map real-world assets using smart contracts.

Neo's base in China allows it unique access to the world's 2nd largest market and the largest cryptocurrency market. This of course is seen as a unique plus when compared to other cryptocurrencies. However current drawbacks include a limited number of wallets for the coin itself, and a lack of ICOs completed on the platform. As of December 2017, there has still only been 1 Neo ICO in the form of Red Pulse.

At the Microsoft China event - Srikanth Raju, GM, Developer Experience & Evangelism and Chief Evangelist, Greater China Region, Microsoft, said that ONCHAIN is "one of the top 50 startup companies in China." Support and positive press from a global powerhouse like Microsoft can only be a positive for Neo going forward.

Perhaps the biggest determining factor for NEO going forward is support from the Chinese government. While other cryptocurrencies suffer from legal battles with governments, Neo's relationship with the leadership has been low key if somewhat positive, with founder Da Hongfei attending government conferences and seminars on cryptocurrency and blockchain technology. After China banned Chinese citizens from participating in ICOs in July 2017, the entire cryptocurrency market took a hit. Neo has the potential to change this. For example, a future ruling that ICOs built on Neo are legal in China would likely see Neo's popularity increase on a worldwide scale.

One thing to be wary of with Neo is once again, a Chinese factor. This time it's the language barrier, as much of the news about the coin is published in Chinese originally, there is significant potential for mistranslations in the English speaking world. For example, "partnerships" with Microsoft and Alibaba (China's largest eCommerce company) have been overstated due to poor translations from Chinese news sources. That doesn't mean collaborations like this aren't possible in the future, but you should always be wary of news coming out of China, especially where unofficial translations are involved.

In the commonly held Neo versus Ethereum debate, there is no reason why one coin has to "win" against the other. Blockchain technology increases in popularity year by year, and there is no reason that both projects cannot coexist. In the short-term at least I would expect DApps to be built on both platforms.

The smart contracts running on Neo include equities, creditor claims, bills and currencies. This also includes the ability to issue what is known as "digital identities", this is paramount if things like financial assets need to be registered on the platform, because it acts a failsafe and holds people accountable if they break the terms of agreements they have set up. These identities will use internationally agreed upon standards, and as such will be compliant in the eyes of regulators. This may contradict many people's idea of completely private blockchain transactions, where identities of all parties are anonymous, but total privacy is not needed for *all* blockchain projects.

Neo has a number of developments planned for 2018, including NEOX, which will be Neo's version of atomic swaps and allow users to swap cryptocurrencies seamlessly without the need for an exchange. As of December 2017 though, this is still very much in the testing stage and the Neo team have not yet completed an atomic swap using NEOX. There are also several more ICOs planned for the platform.

It should also be noted for investing reasons, that one unique aspect of Neo, is that unlike most other cryptocurrencies, the coins are not divisible, so the smallest unit you can buy is indeed 1 Neo.

Gas (GAS)

Price at Time of Writing: $26.97

Market Cap at Time of Writing: $231,878,704

Available on:

Fiat: Coinnest (KOR)

BTC: Binance, Poloniex, OKEx

ETH: Poloniex

Where to store:

Note: Some exchanges will note credit your Gas if you hold Neo in their wallet. Binance definitely *does* credit it, but to make sure you should hold Neo in a non-exchange wallet.

If you've heard of Neo (or if you bought my first book back in August when it was trading at ~$7 as Antshares), then you've probably heard of Gas (previously Antcoins).

Gas is the token used to pay for transactions and service fees using the Neo network. So anytime someone sets up a smart contract, then Gas will be used as a means of payment for the network. It should be noted that the network is currently free as a means of garnering adoption in early stages, but this won't always be the case.

Essentially, Gas is the utility of the entire Neo ecosystem. Gas is what powers the Neo blockchain and allows the DApps built on it to function. Neo tokens on the other hand function more like shares in Neo as a whole.

You can earn Gas just by holding Neo in a wallet (so not on an exchange), currently if you hold 1 NEO, it would take approximately 22 years to generate 1 Gas. However, it may well be more profitable just to buy Gas itself. The thinking behind is the based on the Gas:Neo price ratio, which tends to hover between 0.3 to 0.5. However, many analysts believe the long term ratio will actually be closer to 0.8. This makes Gas an interesting play for higher potential gains than Neo itself. Especially as more and more DApps are launched on the Neo network, and these DApps require more Gas to function.

Right now the schedule of Gas produced by the Neo network is scheduled to end after 22 years (when all 100 million Gas tokens will be in circulation.) There is a caveat however as the Neo developers still reserve the right to produce more Gas tokens if necessary. The team also reserve the right to adjust the amount of Gas required to use the network, however, this should not impact the price of Gas in theory (as they can simply divide the required price into fractions).

Right now the main issues with Gas prices have been that it is not as widely available on exchanges as Neo. For many months Gas was only available to buy on Chinese exchanges, and even at the time of writing, it only available on Binance and Poloniex. So let's make this entirely clear, due to the laws of supply and demand - **it is completely possible for Gas to be worth more than Neo in the short term.**

Stellar Lumens (XLM)

Price at Time of Writing: $0.28

Market Cap at Time of Writing: $5,064,226,845

Available on:

BTC: Bittrex, Binance, Kraken

ETH: Bittrex, Binance

Where to store:

A full selection of wallets including mobile, desktop and web-based are available on

https://www.stellar.org/lumens/wallets/

XLM tokens are also compatible with the Ledger Nano S hardware wallet.

A late bloomer that saw some big price rises at the very end of 2017. Stellar Lumens is an intriguing project with a rather interesting history behind it.

Drawing obvious comparisons to Ripple, the Stellar network is focused on payment processing between large corporations and in the consumer to consumer space. The main difference however is that Stellar operates as a nonprofit organization that doesn't charge for use of the network. The initial funding for the project was from payment processor Stripe.

For example, you are an American who wants to send money to your friend who lives in Germany. Currently, you would have to pay large transaction fees to send Euros from your US bank. However, by using XLM (or Lumens, the currency of the Stellar network). You could send USD, and your friend could withdraw money in Euros, without having to pay huge currency conversion fees. The current base fee for a transaction is just 0.00001 XLM, which is just a fraction of a penny, which is paid for by the sender. Like other blockchain projects, transactions on the Stellar network are publicly available and verifiable to prevent fraud occurring.

The Stellar team also focus on social causes, such as making saw a banking system is available to those who don't currently have access to one. The reduced fees, especially for those who need to frequently send money overseas, is a big selling point in the third world countries this initiative is targeting.

2017 was a big year for the Stellar project, Forbes magazine dubbed it "Venmo, but on a global scale - and for larger bodies like banks and corporations." The coin was added to larger exchanges like Binance and is now compatible with well known hardware wallet including the Ledger Nano S.

In October, the team announced a formal partnership with IBM and KickEx to "develop a blockchain-based cross-border payments solution proven to significantly reduce transaction costs and increase transaction speeds." This announcement kick started a price surge for Stellar which continued for the remainder of the year.

Stellar's history is one that should be mentioned as well. It was founder in 2014 by Jeb McCaleb and Joyce Kim. McCaleb has history in the cryptocurrency space and was one of the founders of the Mt. Gox exchange, which at its peak was the largest cryptocurrency exchange in the world. McCaleb sold the exchange in 2011, shortly before the hacking incident that would result in Mt. Gox's bankruptcy.

McCaleb then moved on to Ripple, but was made to leave the team after the Mt. Gox incident which deterred major financial institutions from wanting to deal with the project. This is where it gets dicey, after being asked, McCaleb announced that he would be liquidating his 9 billion XRP that he accumulated for his part in the project. He proceeded to do so in one lump sum and resulted in XRP's price crashing. He was then taken to court by Ripple and ended up losing the case.

This doesn't necessarily mean anything for Stellar going forward, and the project has been free of any controversy thus far. However I do feel it is important to take a look at the backgrounds of prominent team members, especially those with a track record like McCaleb's.

Moving into 2018, the success of Stellar Lumens will largely depend on the continued adoption of the platform. Partnerships with groups such as SatoshiPay, a web payment system that helps online publishers monetize their content is one such initiative. As of December 2017, the network was processing roughly 30,000 transactions per day with an average transaction time of 4 seconds.

The network does have built-in inflation to deal with the increasing volume of transactions. Currently, this rate is set at 1% per year. 5% of all Lumens (5 billion) are reserved for operating the network.

Groestlcoin (GRS)

Price at Time of Writing: $2.14

Market Cap at Time of Writing: $147,727,132

Available on:

Fiat: Litebit.EU (EUR)

BTC: Bittrex, Cryptopia, Livecoin

ETH: CoinExchange

LTC: Cryptopia

Where to store:

Wallets are available from https://www.groestlcoin.org/downloads/

The rather strangely named Groestlcoin (pronounced "Grow-es-tul coin"), based off an Austrian word meaning quality and rigor, the coin has drawn comparisons to both Litecoin and Vertcoin. GRS is actually a pioneer in cryptocurrency in that it was the first coin to successfully utilize SEGWIT activation back in January 2017.

One of the key components of GRS is how easy it is to mine. If you've read any of my previous books, you'll know that I'm generally against at-home, consumer level mining for larger coins like Bitcoin and Ethereum, due high startup costs, electricity wastage and decreasing ROI year on year. However, GRS has seemingly found a workaround to this issue with their unique mining algorithm.

In their own words "You can mine with your old laptop and still turn over a profit", and power costs are far lower than mining larger coins, and the computer hardware needed is nowhere near as expensive.

In terms of actual use cases, GRS will function mainly for peer-to-peer transactions like Litecoin. There is also a privacy element (similar to Monero), by using the official   Samurai wallet, users can use completely anonymous addresses with 256 bit encryption.

The coin also has a large number of available wallets (which many larger coins are still struggling with), including ones for less popular platforms like Blackberry and Linux. There are also plans to get hardware wallet support in early 2018.

One of the main determinants of the GRS price going forward will be the popularity of atomic swaps. This is a function where users can do coin-to-coin swaps for minimal transaction fees. Uptake of atomic swaps would allow users to exchange coins without having to rely on a centralized exchange.

Funnily enough, one of the sticking points in the GRS community is the name itself. There is a planned rebranding vote, with G2Coin being the most popular alternative suggestion right now. However, as of the time of writing, Groestlcoin remains the name, and GRS the symbol on exchanges.

Ultimately the success of GRS is in much the vein as the other "payment coins" such as Litecoin and Vertcoin. Can their features prove enough to reach wider adoption, especially in the face of mounting Bitcoin dominance in the space, which only appears to be getting stronger. After all, getting merchants or ecommerce stores to accept one crypto payment is one thing, but adopting 4 or 5 at once is whole other story. That being said, GRS is certainly one to watch based on the atomic swap factor alone.

Substratum (SUB)

Price at Time of Writing: $0.56

Market Cap at Time of Writing: $128,717,705

Available on:

BTC: Binance, HitBTC, KuCoin

ETH: Binance, HitBTC, EtherDelta

Where to store:

Substratum is an ERC20 token and can be stored using MyEtherWallet

Substratum is a blockchain project that focuses on the reallocation of unused computer resources. This has many applications such as web hosting and providing storage space for databases. Substratum aims to target both the institutional and consumer markets.

The main difference between this project and traditional cloud hosting services like Amazon Web Services or Rackspace, is that rather than paying for total uptime, users would pay per click on their site. So if you decide to host an unpopular website that doesn't get my traction, you won't be spending excess money on hosting that you don't need.

The platform also promises to be censorship free, so there would be no external monitoring or geo-restrictions in place. This is especially important in the times of net neutrality, where governments give internet service providers that right to charge more to access certain content.

The leads to the question of dealing with content that is deemed morally or legally bad such as terrorism or child pornography. As the network is decentralized, no single person or group has the ability to restrict what can or cannot be seen. Substratum users can vote to remove content from the network if it is deemed obscene or illegal. This voting system would be weighted so that it cannot be manipulated for personal gain by certain groups.

This is the area of the project that has come under the most scrutiny so far. Is a simple voting system enough or keep illegal content from being hosted? Following on, is there a potential workaround to this that doesn't involve a centralized body being in charge of what can and cannot be hosted on the network. Without a doubt, this is the biggest challenge the Substratum project faces in the short term.

Hosting on Substratum can be done by anyone with an internet connection, and hosts would be paid per click as well. The plans are for hosts to be able to run their service or "nodes" in the background without any disruption to their computer's performance. These nodes would be dynamic, so if you are not using your computer, it would allocate more resources to hosting, and vice versa.

For web users, they won't know the difference, it'll just be like viewing any other web page.

The SUB token (known as Substrates) can be used to pay for hosting on the network, but a unique element is that it is not locked into the Substratum ecosystem. By integrating with CryptoPay, users can convert any unused SUB, or SUB they earn from hosting, into different cryptocurrencies or fiat currency, directly through the Substratum website. This kind of dynamic payment system is useful when compared to other cryptocurrency projects that force you to be locked into their particularly token, with no way of converting it without going onto a third party exchange.

Going forward, there are plans to release a public beta version of the platform in Q1 2018, and it will be extremely interesting to see how this goes, especially when related to the points above about hosting dubious content. If it can find a way to effectively deal with this, then there is no doubt in my mind that this project has a lot of room to grow going forward.

Modum (MOD)

Price at Time of Writing: $2.26

Market Cap at Time of Writing: $41,207,269

Available on:

BTC: Binance, Mercatox, Kucoin

ETH: Binance, EtherDelta

Where to store:

Modum is an ERC20 token running on the Ethereum blockchain, therefore it can be stored in MyEtherWallet.

Based out of Switzerland, Modum is a blockchain project that focuses on the supply chain management sector. It aims to provide a monitoring solution for transactions involving physical goods. The first industry Modum is targeting in the Pharmaceutical industry, which spends an approximate $3 billion a year on supply chain monitoring. Modum believes their solution could reduce shipping costs within the industry by as much as 60%.

What Modum does is monitor environmental conditions in the transit of goods. As many pharmaceuticals need specific conditions in order for the product to maintain its use (such as being refrigerated during transportation), it is vital that these conditions are met, and if they are not, it is equally vital that one of the parties be held accountable.

By using smart contracts, Modum allows companies to do this passively. For example, company A is purchasing drug X, which will be shipped from company B's warehouse. Drug X needs to be kept under 4 degrees centigrade during transit to maintain usability. By using Modum smart contracts, company A can verify that the drug was indeed kept under this temperature during transit, and when it arrived at company A's headquarters, a notification will go out, and payment will automatically be released. All of this can be monitored on both desktop and smartphone applications, in addition to a full range of backend data analytics.

The pharmaceutical industry is a wonderful test case as it requires great deal of supply chain integrity, and features a large amount of automation. The industry also has some of the highest standards required for product safety and security, so it's definitely a case of starting at the deep end for the Modum team.

Modum's main challenge is finding adoption from companies who would rather use Modum's solution as opposed to building their own in-house blockchain. Large corporate entities including IBM and Microsoft, are both dedicating large amounts of money to blockchain solutions of their own. It is worth noting that Modum's aim isn't to compete which large scale logistics operators, but to partner up with them and potentially license Modum devices to these larger companies for a best of both worlds solution.

Modum has obviously drawn comparisons to other blockchain projects such as WaltonChain, WaBi and VeChain, however, this isn't necessarily a bad thing. Supply chain management may well be the first widespread use case of blockchain technology. Therefore it's more than possible that all of these coins can co-exist. Modum is the only one of these projects based in Europe, a continent that has a whopping $1.2 trillion pharmaceutical industry.

In the short term, Q1 2018 should see the release of the first of Modum's product line, and an official entry into the Swiss market. The Modum also plans to step up their marketing efforts, which have been relatively lacking thus far. In the longer term, a real time tracking device is currently scheduled for Q1 2019, making Modum a project with long term viability as opposed to just short term monetary gains. Beyond the next couple of years, there is no reason that Modum cannot branch out beyond the pharmaceutical industry into supply chain management for other industries such as clothing. In a world full of hype and talks of 10X price increases in 1 month, I personally like Modum as a long-term hold with actual industry disruption possibilities.

One more interesting thing to note is that although Modum raised approximately $13 million worth of BTC and ETH during their ICO, due to the recent market bull run, this value has actually doubled since. Seeing as the team confirmed in December 2017 that they didn't yet sell any of their BTC or ETH received in the ICO, they have a larger pot to play with going into 2018, which could well see an accelerated roadmap moving forward.

XtraBytes (XBY)

Price at Time of Writing: $0.15

Market Cap at Time of Writing: $65,083,510

Available on:

BTC: Cryptopia, YoBit, C-Cex

LTC: Cryptopia

Where to store:

XtraBytes can be stored in wallets downloaded from https://www.xtrabytes.global/#wallet

XtraBytes aims to provide a decentralized cryptocurrency without dependency on inefficient, centralized mining operations. The projects will do this by using a newly created mining algorithm known as ZOLT which uses a Proof of Signature (PoSIGN) consensus method, as opposed to Proof of Work or Proof of Stake. The project has gathered some steam within the past few months and was the subject of an article on respected cryptocurrency website cointelegraph.com titled "Has XTRABYTES Already Rendered The Top Cryptocurrencies Obsolete?"

While that may be an overstatement at this stage of its development, the project is certainly an interesting one with a huge vision. A network of instant transactions, that are scalable combined with decentralized applications (DApps) that you can program in any language is an appealing proposition.

One of the first apps planned for the XBY ecosystem is X-Change, a decentralized cryptocurrency exchange. This will allow users to trade directly on the blockchain itself, without having to register for a third party exchange. This prevents incidents such as a centralized server being hacked, and user funds being stolen, like was the case with Mt. Gox exchange back in 2014.

Another planned project is X-Vault, a decentralized data storage applications that would store user data in encrypted pieces or "shards" across the network. This would prevent anyone from being able to access user data because even if they could "hack" one part of the network, they would only be able to access a tiny portion of the data. There are also additional plans for a decentralized instant messaging service as well as a platform for designed and executing smart contracts.

Currently, the project has managed to perform over 1,000 transactions per second on the TestNet, with a theoretical maximum of over 10,000 transactions per second. For comparison, Ethereum currently does around 20 transactions per second, albeit on a larger scale. Visa currently handles around 1,800 transactions per second.

XtraBytes has a long way to go before it can compete with larger projects in a similar vein like Cardano and EOS. A successful launch of both X-Change and X-Vault, even in beta form is likely to have positive price action as we move forward. A concentrated marketing effort is also needed if the coin is to receive more traction. It is important to note that much XBY's technology is still either in testing or theoretical stage, which explains its lower price and marketcap compared to some of the other projects mentioned here. However, a project with as much potential as this one should absolutely be on your radar in 2018 and beyond.

RaiBlocks (XRB)

Price at Time of Writing: $3.28

Market Cap at Time of Writing: $436,917,146

Available on:

BTC: BitGrail, Mercatox, BitFlip

Where to store:

Online wallets are available from https://raiwallet.com/

Other desktop wallets are available on the official website https://raiblocks.net/

Currently hardware wallet support is planned for Q1 2018

RaiBlocks aims to use blockchain technology to facilitate peer-to-peer transactions in a fast, costless manner. RaiBlocks does this by using an unconventional blockchain variant known as a "block-lattice", in which easy user runs their own blockchain, known as an "account-chain", which allows for faster transactions. The ultimate goal is for XRB to become a fast, feeless way for a regular person to move their money around. This has led to XRB being dubbed "Blockchain 3.0" by some commentators.

Since each user runs their own account chain, both the sender and the recipient are required to confirm the transaction, unlike the traditional model which only requires confirmation from the sender. Although for convenience, the recipient of the transaction can confirm it at a later date, so it doesn't require them to be online at the time the transaction is sent.

One of the major advantages of this model is that transaction are infinitely scalable in theory because individual transactions settle regardless of other network activity. Therefore there is no "transaction queue", which we have seen with other cryptocurrencies, notably Bitcoin. This also means traditional mining algorithms like Proof of Work, are not necessary to verify the transaction.

Another major advantage of this model compared a traditional one, is the overall security of the network. In theory, one could take down the entire Bitcoin or Litecoin network without owning a single dollar worth of either currency. With XRB, you would need to own 51% of all the XRB in the world to coordinate such an attack, making it not only financially pointless but also a waste of time from a moral or ethical standpoint. After all, why would you want to take down a network that you own the majority of?

RaiBlocks price going forward will largely be determined by the team's ability to get on major exchanges. With the majority of the volume currently traded on BitGrail, which is a relatively tiny exchange when compared to giants like Binance and Bittrex. Long time price determinants will be mass adoption, both on a peer-to-peer basis, and for a consumer-to-business payment system. The latter is something many coins are trying to achieve, and it is unlikely there is space for all of them going forward. It remains to be seen how much of that space XRB will take up, and as such, it should be viewed as a speculative investment.

In terms of competitor coins, IOTA is the obvious one, as their missions are largely the same, and neither of them requires any kind of mining or mining resources. However, RaiBlocks does have an advantage in that their network doesn't require Proof of Work to maintain security, and thus their long term costs are much lower. Another major difference is that XRB allows you to reuse addresses for transactions, an issue that IOTA faced when a few users lost a lot of currency because they tried to receive IOTA at an address they had already used. It should be noted that nearly every other cryptocurrency allows you to reuse a wallet address, so this is very much an IOTA problem rather than a cryptocurrency problem. There is an additional project in Radix, but it is still largely under development and far behind the other two at this stage.

Nav Coin (NAV)

Price at Time of Writing: $2.63

Market Cap at Time of Writing: $163,670,064

Available on:

Fiat: LiteBit.eu (EUR)

BTC: Bittrex, Poloniex, Cryptopia

LTC: Cryptopia

Where to store:

You can download wallets from https://navcoin.org/downloads/ - by using these wallets you can stake your coins and earn 5% interest on them

Based out of New Zealand and dubbed "The world's first fully anonymous cryptocurrency", Nav coin is one of the older projects around having started in 2014 as a fork of Bitcoin with greater optimization. For example Nav transaction times are around 30 seconds as opposed to Bitcoin's 10 minutes, as well as optional anonymous transactions. Nav also has low transactions fees, which currently amount to around $0.03 per transaction.

Nav's anonymity element is interesting because it uses a different anonymity algorithm to other major privacy coins. The two major algorithms in use are CryptoNote/Ring CT, which is used by Monero, and ZKSnarks, which is used by ZCash. These algorithms are both relatively new, and have little literature or regulated studies performed on their security, which is paramount for any network that claims to be anonymous.

Nav on the other hand uses the RSA algorithm, which is the most studied of the three. The RSA algorithm uses 2048 bit length keys, which are near impossible to hack via brute force.

Nav uses Proof of Stake (PoS), as opposed to Proof of Work (PoW). Not only is PoS a more environmentally friendly way of mining, as it doesn't require giant mining farms, it also allows you to earn interest on your coins by "staking" these coins to help run the network. PoS would also require any network attacker to own 51% of the coins themselves in order to coordinate an attack on the network.

Nav's big development move going forward is the release of NavPay and Polymorph. NavPay is a mobile wallet that would allow anonymous transactions between wallets, nothing too special there right? However, when combined with Polymorph, this would allow anonymous transactions of coins through coin transfer programs like Changelly. This is convenient because it allows cryptocurrency to cryptocurrency swaps without having to register for many different online exchanges. You can think of this like atomic swaps, but with an added privacy element. So for example, you could anonymously exchange your LTC to BTC, using Nav as the intermediary currency. So even if your base currencies do not have a privacy element, you could use Nav as the go-between to take advantage of a private transaction.

QASH (QASH)

Price at time of writing - $0.98

Market cap at time of writing - $346,077,200

Available on:

Fiat: Bitfinex, Quoine (USD & JPY)

BTC: Bitfinex, Quoine, Qryptos

ETH: Huobi, Qryptos

Where to store:

You can store QASH using MyEtherWallet by adding it as a custom token. Alternatively, you can store it on the Qryptos exchange in the short term.

QASH (also known as the Quoine Liquid Token) is one of the most interesting cryptocurrency projects as we head in 2018. The Quoine Liquid Platform plans to become the world's premiere cryptocurrency trading platform by combining liquidity from multiple markets.

Currently the global foreign exchange market for traded fiat currencies stands at around $5-6 trillion per day. Cryptocurrency's average trading volume is around $3 billion per day, but continues to grow on a monthly basis. The biggest problem the cryptocurrency market faces however is limited liquidity, especially when we are talking about the lesser known cryptocurrencies. Most cryptocurrencies are only liquid in a few pairings, and this varies from exchange to exchange. For example, there may be a lot of BTC/Neo liquidity on one exchange, but little on another. This also applies to many less used fiat to crypto pairings such as Canadian dollars, New Zealand dollars and Philippine Pesos. Citizens of these countries should all be able to access the cryptocurrency market, but they are currently being limited by lack of volume from their respective currency.

The Quoine Liquid platform plans to solve this problem by aggregating various liquidity sources into one single giant tradable order book. In other words, by combining liquidity from multiple markets, there is now enough to be able to fill everyone's orders. This would also allow buyers to buy cryptocurrency in their currency of choice, without having to convert to a more popular fiat currency first. The end result of this is that users would be able to effectively trade on any global exchange, without having to register or hold funds on that exchange.

QASH aims to become the world's first prime brokerage for cryptocurrency. This means they would offer a multitude of services including securities trading, credit facilities including lending, and leveraged trading. Prime brokerages appeal to institutional clients as well as to consumer clients.

Where the QASH token comes in is as a means of payment for using all services tied to the Quoine Liquid platform, such as transaction fees, as well as a token that is tradable on the open market like other cryptocurrencies. QASH holders will receive a 5% discount for transactions on the platform, with no maximum limit. This is especially important when we factor in prime brokerages into this, because a 5% discount on a transaction of $50,000,000 (not uncommon for prime brokerages), represents huge savings to the client.

QASH will initially be built on the Ethereum blockchain using ERC-20 tokens. Going forward, the team plans to migrate the project onto their own blockchain in mid 2019.

One of the major advantages of QASH is that the Liquid platform is already complete and online. At the time of writing the platform supports 15 different cryptocurrencies. The platform is fully licensed and regulated by the Japan Financial Services Agency.

The big growth factor for QASH and the Liquid Platform going forward will be adoption from institutional clients. If their first to market approach is successful, they could see an influx of large clients from Asia and beyond and this would provide them with a significant advantage of their competition. This alone makes QASH a cryptocurrency to watch as we move into 2018.

Cardano (ADA)

Price at time of writing - $0.50

Market cap at time of writing - $13,003,955,572

Available on:

Fiat: Coinnest (ROK)

BTC: Bittrex, Binance

ETH: Binance, Bittrex

Where to store:

You can store Cardano using their official Daedulus Wallet https://daedaluswallet.io/ - please note, at the time of writing there is an unofficial Daedulus Wallet listed on the Google Play Store. **For safety precautions do not download any Cardano wallets from the Google Play Store**

Cardano aims to become the world's most advanced open source smart contract platform. It can also boast of being the first ever cryptocurrency project that has been completed peer reviewed by a group of academic researchers. Cardano is built using the Haskell programming language, a language that is not often used in cryptocurrency projects, but one that can be considered one of the more secure, and least prone to errors.

Cardano can be seen as the 3rd generation of cryptocurrency, in that the project aims to revolutionize how we see blockchain technology as a whole by developing what the Cardano team believes is a fairer and more balanced ecosystem. This is opposed to first generation cryptocurrency like Bitcoin that merely function as a peer-to-peer monetary transaction system. On important distinction to make is that while other cryptocurrencies began as, and continue to be a work in progress, Cardano took the decisions to work on the project behind the scenes, and bringing to market a protocol that would be able to handle future adaptation.

The project uses a unique Proof of Stake (PoS) mining algorithm known as Ouroboros, as opposed to a Proof of Work algorithm.

An important element of the Cardano project is what they term the "social element of money", in other words, how particular communities interact with their money. This makes sense if you think about the broader scale of different cryptocurrencies. For example, Bitcoin and Litecoin have very few technical differences between them, the same goes for Ethereum and Ethereum Classic. However, all 4 of these cryptocurrencies still maintain large communities supporting them and each of them have large market capitalizations.

Where Cardano comes in is the ability for users to propose changes in how their cryptocurrency of choice operates. This could be from voting on which projects the development team devotes funds to, to how different markets should be regulated. Cardano does this by utilizing a decentralized trust fund, which will be collected from transaction fees on the network. In theory, any user can request funds from the trust, and a ballot system would be used to decide whether the request is fulfilled or not. This would solve disputes such as soft or hard fork debates that have adversely affected both the Bitcoin and Ethereum communities.

One of the key elements of Cardano is a balance between the privacy of users on the platform and the needs of regulators such as government bodies.

Cardano is very much a long term project, and the roadmap signals that the full platform is not scheduled for release until early 2019. Investing in a project without a working product is a high risk move, and if you do choose to invest in Cardano, you should do your due diligence before allocating any of your portfolio towards it.

Bitcoin Cash (BCH/BCC)

Price at time of writing - $3,547.70

Market cap at time of writing - $59,829,341,444

Exchanges:

Fiat: Coinbase (as of 12/20/17), BitHumb (ROK), Coinone (ROK), Kraken

BTC: Bittrex, Bitfinex, Poloniex

Where to store:

There are numerous wallets available for all platforms on http://bitcoincash.org

Bitcoin Cash is also supported by both Trezor and Ledger Nano S hardware wallets.

I suppose we should probably talk about Bitcoin Cash. Especially for those of you who are new to the market and are wondering why on Earth there are now 2 Bitcoins on Coinbase (as of 12/20/17). I've already discussed Bitcoin Cash in my first book, *Cryptocurrency: Beginners Bible,* however as there have been a number of major developments since then, I felt it would have been a disservice not to provide an updated version of my summary.

Bitcoin Cash (BCH) emerged as the result of a split or "hard fork" in the Bitcoin technology on August 1st 2017. The end-goal of Bitcoin Cash is to function as a global currency, in the founder's words, to be what Bitcoin was supposed to have been in line with the original vision for Bitcoin outlined in the 2008 whitepaper.

If you held Bitcoin before August 1st (or to be technical, all Bitcoin holders as of block 478558), you will have been credited with an equal amount of Bitcoin Cash. Coinbase finally did this on 12/20/17, the same day that Bitcoin Cash was added. Your BCH will have been deposited directly into your wallet. It should be noted however that not all exchanges credited user accounts with BCH, so it's worth double checking yours.

The split occurred out of problems with Bitcoin's ability to process transactions at a high speed. For example, the Visa network processes around 1,700 transactions per second whereas Bitcoin averages around 7. As the network continues to grow, so do waiting times for transactions. BCC aims to run more transactions, as well as, providing lower transactions fees.

One of the major solutions to this issue is increasing the size of each block, so that more data can be processed at once. Bitcoin Cash increases the block size to 8MB, as opposed to the 1MB size of Bitcoin. This is in line with solving the problems of scalability that Bitcoin was facing previously. The technology itself worked in the short-term, with the first Bitcoin Cash block registering 7,000 transactions compared with Bitcoin's 2,500.

The success of failure of Bitcoin Cash will largely depend on Bitcoin's own adoption of the SegWit technology, and the ability to process transactions quicker to act truly as a currency - rather than a speculative asset. Detractors have also raised security concerns about Bitcoin Cash.

Bitcoin Cash has been widely adopted by many cryptocurrency exchanges. At the time of writing, there are only a few months worth of data available and thus, no one has been able to execute any long-term trends or technical analysis of BCH as a commodity. As further adoption continues, the price may well continue to rise. Early price rises for Bitcoin Cash have been largely driven by demand from South Korea, with over 50% of the total trade volume being seen on South Korean exchanges.

There are also now two divided camps within the Bitcoin movement, with the original Bitcoin (or Bitcoin Core) on one side, and Bitcoin Cash on the other.

Miners have been quick to adopt the currency as well due to its higher mining ROI when compared to Bitcoin. The decrease in mining difficulty (leading to greater rewards for mining) will continue to see for miners move their resources from Bitcoin into Bitcoin Cash.

As we move into 2018, arguably the biggest debate in the cryptocurrency community will be whether Bitcoin and Bitcoin Cash can co-exist, or if one will win out against the other. Once it was added to Coinbase, Bitcoin Cash once again reached near all time highs in value compared to Bitcoin, but 2018 will be a big year in determining if BCH is here to stay.

Note: Depending on your exchange, Bitcoin Cash may use the symbol BCC or BCH - double check before executing a trade

How to Identify Market Manipulation

When investing in any cryptocurrency, it's important to be aware of market manipulation in the form of coordinated pump and dump schemes. This is more prevalent with lower volume cryptocurrencies where manipulation is easier to perform.

It doesn't take much digging to find the groups behind these, a few Google searches bring up various groups on Telegram, a Russian cloud-based instant messenger app that encrypts users identities. These groups aren't exactly subtle about their intentions with names such as Crypto4Pumps and PumpKing. These groups coordinate mass buys of low cap cryptocurrencies to artificially inflate the price, then sell their holding at a higher price once the general public become aware of it.

The reason these schemes can exist is the lack of regulation in the cryptocurrency market. These schemes used to be prevalent in the form of email blasts, during the penny stock market craze back in the mid 2000s, before many of the largest groups were shut down by regulators like the SEC.

The groups release buy signals to their users ahead of time, who then prepare funds, before being alerted to which cryptocurrency to buy. Previous coins that have been targets of these include MagiCoin, Gnosis and Ubiq. Once the initial buys happen, the group moves to other channels to "spread the word" of a great buying opportunity.

The initial buyers are now ready to dump their coins at a profit, which then tanks the price of the coin. Leaving those who bought late at a huge loss.

So how can you avoid these? Simply look at volumes on exchanges, and if you see a tiny market cap coin with a giant increase then stay well away. Price rises of 50% in under an hour are not uncommon with these sorts of schemes. Most major exchanges allow you to sort by price increase in the past hour, and it's a metric worth looking at. So don't chase anything purely because you see a quick price rise and hope to get in on the action, chances are you are already too late. Remember to do your own research before investing in a coin, and invest without emotion or the hope of instant riches.

One big cryptocurrency to avoid - why you should be wary of Bitconnect

Bitconnect, which trades as BCC on many exchanges, should be avoided in my opinion. I make careful choices never to go out of my way to specifically recommend coins worth buying, and this book is my personal opinion and not financial advice.

However, I will take a stance against any cryptocurrency project that I believe gives the space a bad name, and Bitconnect does just that. Currently ranked #20 on CoinMarketCap.com with a total market cap of $1.7 billion, the project is heavily promoted on social media. Bitconnect has a huge a number of red flags around the project and I've laid them out below.

Red Flag 1: Bitconnect is a Bitcoin lending system that promises enormous gains for those who put money into the platform. Their website promises returns of 1% *per day,* which anyone with any understanding of finance will tell you is impossible to uphold in the long term without completely breaking the world's economy.

Red Flag 2: Bitconnect claims their trading bots will continuously make money in order to fulfill these returns, regardless of overall market conditions. If they really did have a bot capable of doing this, why would they need investors? Surely that complicates things and adds unnecessary risk for them?

Red Flag 3: A capital "lock up" period of 299 days. So every investor *must* keep their initial investment in the Bitconnect program for 299 days before being allowed to cash out. That seems fishy as other managed funds do not require this or any other sort of "minimum investment period".

Red Flag 4: No public blockchain transactions that can verify their trading bots effectiveness. This is blockchain after all, so why can't we see how well the bot is doing? Their marketing video doesn't mention the bot very much, because they concentrate more on how rich everyone involved in the project is.

Red Flag 5: Bitconnect was originally registered in the UK, but the company was shut down because it never filed any accounts.

Red Flag 6: Prominent cryptocurrency figures including Ethereum Founder Vitalik Buterin, Litecoin founder Charlie Lee, and billionaire blockchain investor Michael Novogratz have dismissed the project as a "Ponzi scheme" and "most likely a scam."

Red Flag 7: This is the big one. Their referral system. Bitconnect operates a 7 layer referral bonus system. A system where you receive a % bonus from your referrals, and a smaller percentage from their referrals, and then an even smaller percentage from their referral's referrals. Do you see where this is going? Does the phrase "pyramid scheme" spring to mind?

As usual, I encourage you to do your own research on top of what you read in this book. I would be extremely vary of any program in cryptocurrency or otherwise, that promises guaranteed returns, and for that reason along with the others listed above, I strongly urge you to avoid Bitconnect.

Update: On January 17th 2018 - Bitconnect pulled the largest exit scam in cryptocurrency history. The price of BCC tokens plunged from $400 to less than $4 in a few short weeks.

Cryptocurrency Golden Rules for Safety & Security

So now you've bought your coins, here's a guide on how to safely store them, as well as some general best practices to employ with cryptocurrency.

1. Never give your private key to anyone

Your private key is what you need to spend your coins, therefore you are the only one who should hold it. You should keep your private key secure, preferably written down on paper and stored somewhere safe (like a safety deposit box). If your cryptocurrency is stored on an exchange, you likely won't have a private key and will use your exchange password to sell your coins.

2. Do not store your coins on an exchange long-term

No matter how good or reputable an exchange is, because of their centralized nature they are still vulnerable to being hacked. If you have any significant amount of cryptocurrency you should store it either in a desktop, paper or hardware wallet. For each of the coins listed I have provided links to wallets you can store them in. For hardware wallets I recommend the Trezor or Ledger Nano S, although not all coins are compatible with these.

3. Double check all links to websites (including ones in this book)

Phishing scams are still rife in the cryptocurrency space, and unfortunately, some of these links slip through Google Adwords checks and therefore appear at the top of a Google search for that cryptocurrency or exchange. Make sure you check the URL you are typing in or clicking on, so you don't end up on binnance.com or mynetherwallet.com by mistake. This is even more important when it's a website that requires your username and password.

4. **Don't reveal how much cryptocurrency you have**

I see this a lot on social media this days with people posting about their 5, 6 or even 7 figure portfolios. Your identity can be traced back to you if someone really wants to, and if they know you have millions of dollars worth of cryptocurrency, they suddenly have a motivation to do so. To be on the safe side, don't post on the internet regarding the amount of cryptocurrency you own. Posting about which coins you own is perfectly fine though.

5. **Get your news from reputable sources**

When investing in cryptocurrency, it can often be hard to know who to trust. There is a lot of misinformation out there, and this leads to bad investing moves. Unfortunately, mainstream media is particularly bad at reporting cryptocurrency news, preferring to choose soundbites that are attention-grabbing rather than fact-filled. For example, December saw articles stating "CEO of Bitcoin.com sells all his Bitcoin" but many of these articles failed to note that Bitcoin.com is merely a website that allows you to create Bitcoin wallets, and is no way an official Bitcoin operation. Which grossly overstated the event in the eyes of the general public.

I personally recommend cointelegraph.com and coindesk.com for keeping tabs on happenings within the cryptocurrency space.

Finally, never invest more than you can afford to lose, and never borrow money to invest in cryptocurrency.

Conclusion

Well there we have it, a summary of the cryptocurrency market and its direction as we head into 2018. As well as, a list of high potential coins that could have massive growth in the next 12 months and beyond. There has never been a better time to be involved in the world's fastest growing financial market, and if you haven't already invested, I hope this book gives you the confidence to do so.

Remember to only invest what you can afford to lose, and cryptocurrency investments should only make up a small percentage of your overall portfolio. I encourage you to do additional research before you invest your money, and remember to watch out for any nefarious elements like pump and dump schemes.

I wish you the best of luck in the cryptocurrency market, and I hope you make a lot of money.

Thanks,

Stephen

P.S. If you sign up for Coinbase using this link, you will receive $10 worth of free Bitcoin after your first purchase of more than $100 worth of cryptocurrency.

http://bit.ly/10dollarbtc

Cryptocurrency

10 Biggest Trading Mistakes Newbies Make - And How to Avoid Them

By Stephen Satoshi

"Men wanted for hazardous journey. Low wages, bitter cold, long hours of complete darkness. Safe return doubtful. Honor and recognition in event of success."

— Ernest Shackleton.

"Never confuse brains with a bull market"

— Anonymous.

Introduction

So you've decided to take the plunge into the cryptocurrency fast lane. You're looking for those gigantic returns you've read so much about. Well, you've come to the right place. Trading is without a doubt the quickest way to get rich with cryptocurrency.

From the outset though, let's make something clear. Trading is incredibly risky, and you are liable to lose money if you don't know what you're doing. The entire point of this book is avoid making giant mistakes, that losing traders always seem to make. So you can mitigate some of the risk by directing your attention to learning the right trading principles to set you up for long term trading success.

These aren't just technical principles, and I won't have you studying 500 chart patterns for 3 years before investing your first dollar, pounds or euros. There are significant mental preparations you need to make before you begin trading. This applies to cryptocurrencies, as well as any other financial trading situation. You'll also need to learn the principles of money management, and how to correctly use your bankroll to give you the biggest chance of long term trading success.

It is advisable to spend a significant portion of your time studying trading theory before you spend time trading your hard earned coins. Remember, at its very core, trading comes down to two factors, and two factors only.

1. Making money

2. Keeping what you've made

As we're currently in one of the biggest bull markets ever seen, many people are doing number one quite well. However, what remains to be seen is if they'll keep their money once the market turns bearish, and our beloved cryptocurrencies start to drop in price (which is a matter of when, and not if - this is a financial market after all).

Trading is the ultimate rush, it's a game played against one another via a computer screen, where it's your mind against another person, your money against theirs. Some days you come home a conquering hero, and other days you'll be left beaten, demoralized and broken. Hopefully, you'll be having more of the former than the latter after studying this book, and you'll become a consistently profitable trader going forward.

And as per usual: **Only invest what you can afford to lose**

I wish you all the best in your trading endeavors,

Stephen

Trading vs. Investing

For the vast majority of people, buying a coin and holding it for the long term is a smarter move than actively trading one or multiple coins at once. You see, cryptocurrency trading is rife with uninformed "traders" who simply buy and sell on a whim and inevitably end up broke, even in the current bull market conditions. Luckily for you, if you take some time to study the basics, you can outwit and outtrade these people and take consistent profits for yourself.

Trading Cryptocurrency vs. Big Board Stocks or Penny Stocks vs. Forex

If you've dabbled in trading securities before, then you'll probably be familiar with some of the concepts discussed in this book. However, there are a few major differences between trading cryptocurrency and trading traditional stocks or even penny stocks.

The main one of these is that the cryptocurrency market is open 24/7 365. There are no weekends off, there are no market closures at 1PM for holidays or anything like that. As such, traditional trading advice such as "the best time of day to trade" falls by the wayside here. Price movements can happen while you sleep because the Chinese market is already up and trading, or there is a large volume of buy order coming in from Korea. Events like this aren't uncommon, and you need to be aware of these factors before committing to trading.

Mistake 1: Falling for Pump & Dump Schemes

Opt-In Pump & Dump Emails

Another thing to be aware of. These are a hangover from the mid 2000s when penny stock trading was all the rage, and scammy stock promoters would send out emails to their list promoting a certain stock. Either because they were paid to do so by the company, or the promoters had already invested big themselves. They then wait for the email recipients to invest and push the price up even more, before dumping their shares on the market for a profit, leaving the email recipients holding large losses.

Unfortunately, due to the lack of regulation by the SEC, companies regularly do this for cryptocurrency as well. That is why I recommend you don't subscribe to any of these types of emails, whether a free or paid service. Your trading should be done based on market condition and technical analysis, which we'll go into in more depth later on in this book.

Technical Analysis

Mistake 2: Not utilizing technical analysis

Why Technical Analysis is vital in any form of financial trading

1. Future trends follow past trends

Human beings are a predictable bunch, and we generally do the same things over and over again. This also applies to trading, because certain patterns emerge and repeat themselves, and we can use the patterns to somewhat accurately predict price movements.

2. We're all looking at the same charts

Individual human beings are less good at predicting things than a group of humans predicting the same event, the "wisdom of the crowd" if you will. How this relates to cryptocurrency trading is that as there are thousands of us looking at the same chart, we will generally come to the same conclusion and make similar moves to one another.

3. The current cryptocurrency price includes all available data

Even data that isn't widely or publicly available will be factored in (this is the advantage that so-called "insiders") have over the rest of the trading population. Thus, we can assume that the current price of the cryptocurrency is correct.

All technical analysis can be broken down into 2 main chart patterns:

Continuation Patterns - Where the price of a coin is expected to keep trending the same way it is currently moving

Reversal Patterns - Where the price of a coin is expected to reverse from its current trend (I.e. a coin's price is expected to stop falling and start rising)

The following are some of the basic, and most essential chart patterns you need to know. You can get by with an in-depth knowledge of these, and having a deeper knowledge of the basics charts is better than having surface level knowledge of many charts.

For more in-depth reading on technical analysis, I having a recommended reading list at the end of this book.

Support & Resistance

If you're going to learn one technical tool for trading, make it support and resistance levels. These horizontal trend lines are the lifeblood of all technical analysis.

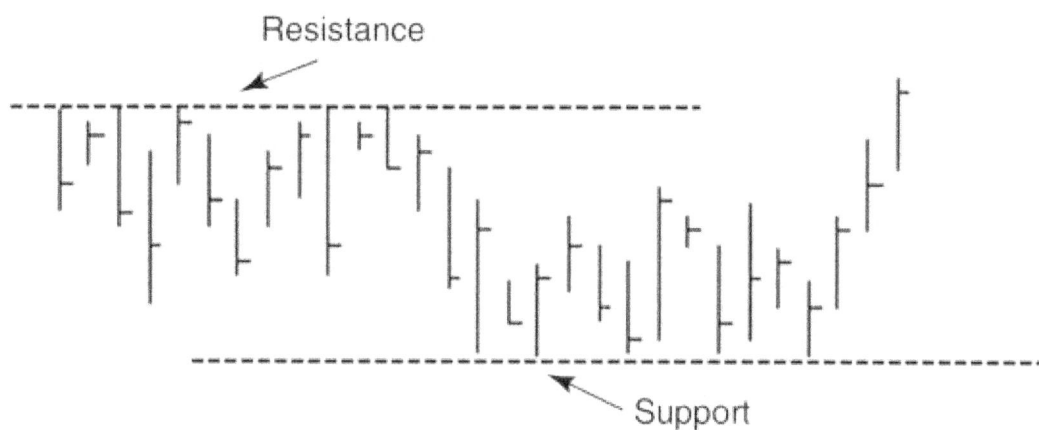

Support Level:

A support level for a coin is a price in which traders do not think it will fall below. They believe there is enough demand at that price that investors will continue to buy, and this will prevent any further declines in the price. Support levels can be identified using charting patterns.

If you're just starting out, study longer term historical data and use this to identify previous support levels for a coin. So with the case of Bitcoin, use 6 month or 12 month graphs rather than 1 week graphs.

Resistance Level:

Resistance level is simply the opposite of a support level. It's a price where traders don't believe there is enough demand to break through and go higher, therefore more traders will be selling at this particular price. Resistance levels are calculated slightly differently than support levels due to the nature of human psychology. For example, round numbers often have a psychological effect e.g. Bitcoin @ $10,000 or ETH @ $300 and this creates a resistance level in itself. You can also use the reverse of the techniques you used to find a support level on a chart.

For both support and resistance levels, look for at least two or three price action zones in a single chart. Once you identify this price action zones, you can draw a straight line to indicate support and resistance levels. Generally speaking, the more a coin hits a specific support or resistance level, the stronger the price move will be once it does finally break through.

Once a stock breaks through it's resistance level, it's not uncommon for the previous resistance level to become the new support level and vice versa. Understanding this helps your risk management as you continue to trade more frequently.

Candlestick Charting

Candlestick charting, also called Japanese candlesticks is one of the best ways to determine support and resistance levels in a coin. Candlesticks take into account the opening, closing, high and low price of that particular day for a coin.

There are literally hundreds of different candlestick patterns you can learn, but there are a few that are absolutely vital to know, so those will be the ones we discuss in this book. One more thing to point out when studying candlestick charts. Red or black candlesticks represent downward movement, whereas white or green candlesticks represent upward movement.

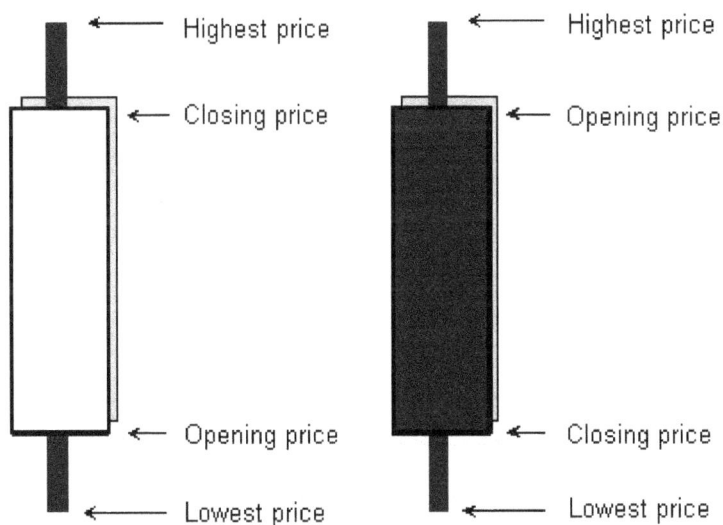

Doji

Doji's are characterized by a very small difference between opening and closing price and look like plus signs on a chart. The Doji pattern represents indecision in the market, these are usually found near support and resistance points, because market participants aren't sure if the coin will break these levels.

When analyzing candlestick charts, you should use daily charts that go back at least 3 months and try to identify patterns.

Channels

Channels are plotted with 2 parallel lines on a candlestick or line chart and denote continued support and resistance levels as a coin is trending in upwards or downwards fashion. Channels are useful because they help us form multiple ideal entry and exit points for a particular coin going forward. This is a big plus if you plan on trading frequently.

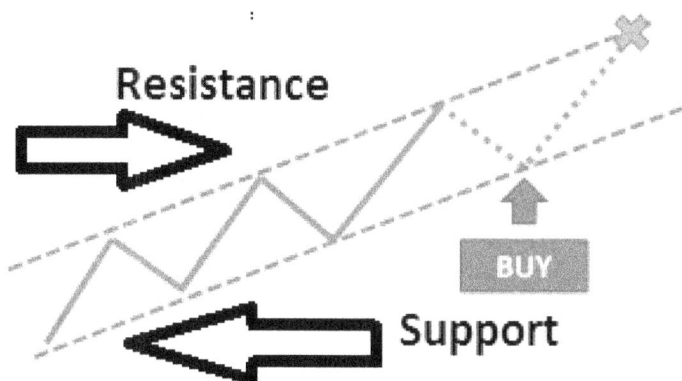

Head & Shoulders Pattern

One of the most important patterns to recognize is the head and shoulders reversal pattern. Simply put this indicates that the trend of the coin is about to reverse. So in the example below, the price is expected to drop. If the chart is inverted, we would expect a rise in price going forward.

The expected price movement (denoted by m in the picture) can be calculated as the inverse of the price between the neckline and the head, which is why it is crucial that you measure the neckline correctly.

Note, the majority of the time, the chart will not be a perfectly aligned head and shoulders, but the general pattern is enough to go on.

Head and Shoulder Top

Left shoulder

Head

Right shoulder

Price

Neckline

Period & volume

Double Top & Double Bottom

A double top (bearish), and its inverse the double bottom (bullish), are made up of 2 consecutive peaks with a trough in-between. Most of the time the first peak will be slightly higher than the second peak and be accompanied by a higher volume as well.

It is also not uncommon for there to be a triple top or triple bottom pattern if there is not enough volume to break through resistance or support levels. Like most patterns, once a breakthrough occurs, the previous support level becomes the new resistance level and vice versa.

The double top is one pattern that newer traders often misinterpret, especially when looking at short term charts. Remember to focus on volume at the support/resistance levels before entering a trade.

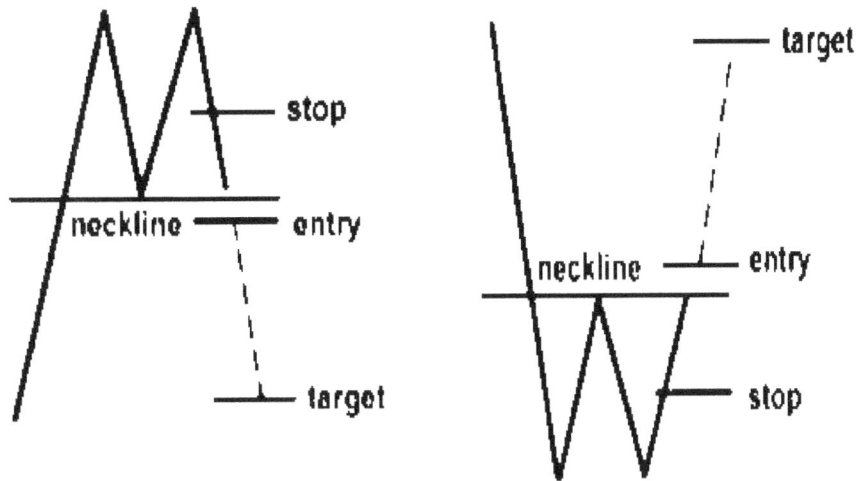

Double Top and Double Bottom

Triangles

We could probably write an entire book just on various triangle based patterns, but we'll stick to the basics here. The three types of triangle pattern are the symmetrical, ascending and descending triangle.

Symmetrical Triangle

A symmetrical triangle is a continuation pattern that signals a price is going to keep moving in the same direction after a brief trend reversal. The two points of the triangle start from the support and resistance lines then converge. The price of the coin has been trading between these two lines and then will continue to trend in the previous direction once these lines meet.

Ascending Triangle

An ascending triangle is a bullish pattern that signals the price will keep moving upwards after a period of bouncing around the resistance line, but not dipping low enough to hit the support line. The line is drawn from the previous resistance and support lines, and will converge at the resistance line. If there is enough volume, the price will break the resistance line and continue to rise.

Descending Triangle

The opposite of the ascending triangle is a bearish pattern, except this time the lines converge at the support level. Enough volume at this level will result in a breakthrough to lower prices.

Symmetrical Triangle   Ascending Triangle   Descending Triangle

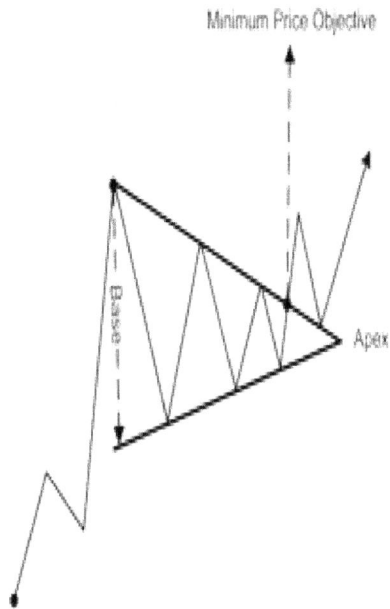

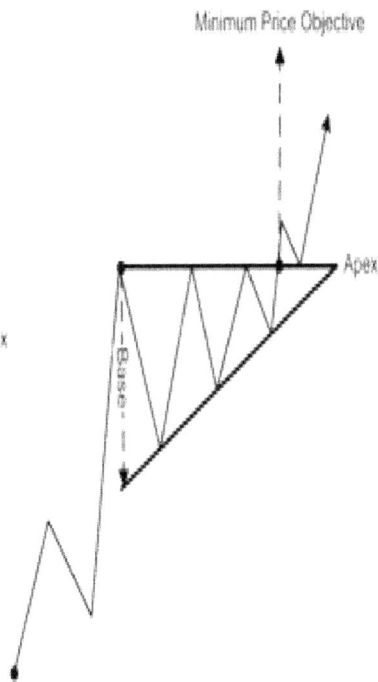

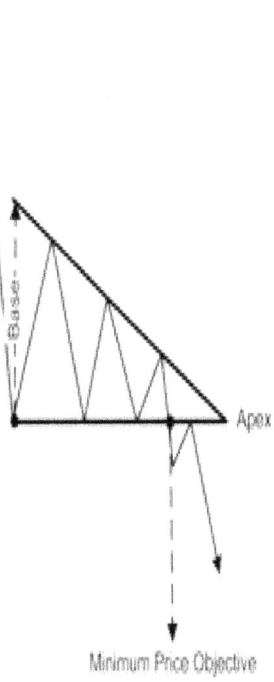

Minimum Price Objective   Minimum Price Objective

Base   Base   Base

Apex   Apex   Apex

Minimum Price Objective

Flag Patterns

Flag patterns are similar to triangle patterns that appear during consolidation period (small reversal from previous price movements). They are represented by two parallel lines following a of a sharp price movement (which acts as the flag "mast") Following a flag patterns, prices continue to trend in the same direction they were moving previously.

The slope of the flag will be the opposite direction to the predicted price movement, so a downward sloping flag will signal a continued bull movement, and an upward sloping flag will signal a continued bear movement.

Like triangle patterns, the buy or sell signal comes when there is enough volume to break through the previous support or resistance level.

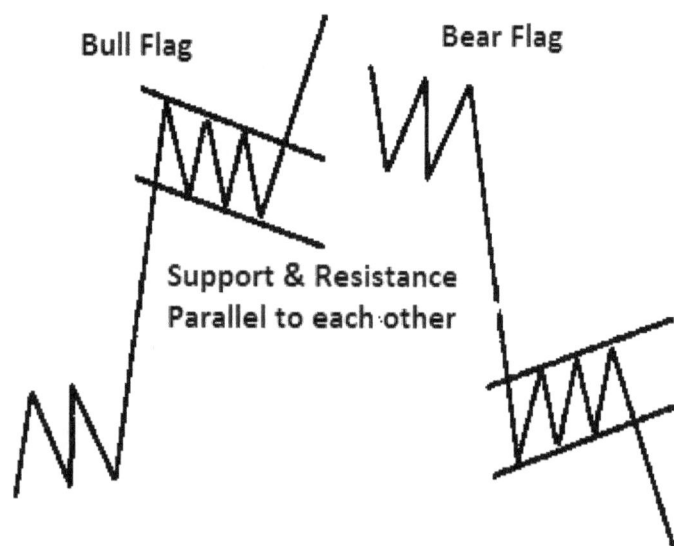

Bull Flag

Bear Flag

Support & Resistance Parallel to each other

The Baseball Cap

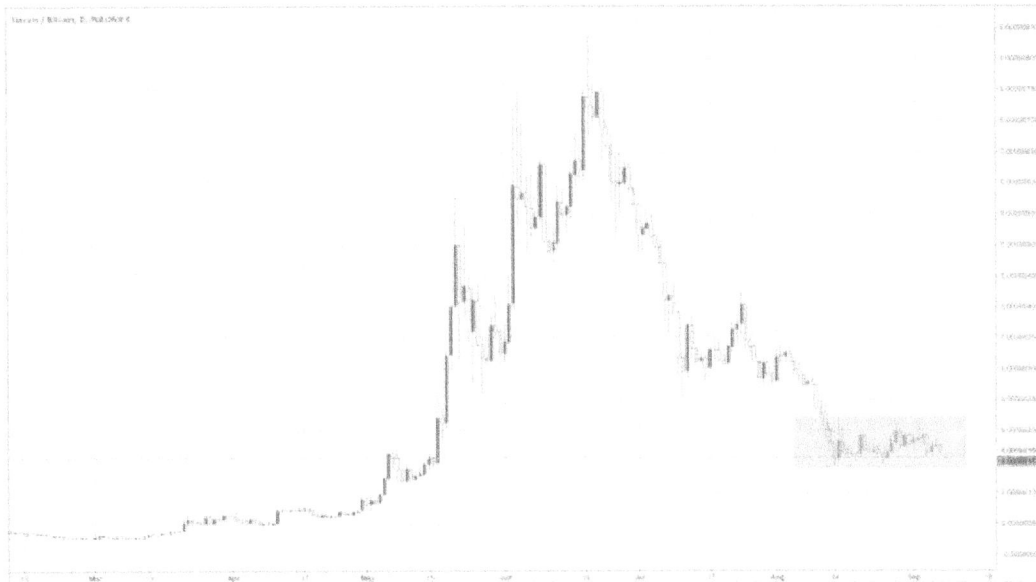

The Baseball cap is a consolidation pattern where a new support level forms after a dip in price. This new "floor price" means the price has stabilized for the time being, and due to the cyclical and high volatility nature of cryptocurrencies, this is usually followed a sharp increase in price. Like in the chart below. If you study the baseball cap pattern enough, then you can time you buys correctly - and therefore if you're going to learn one pattern well - make it this one.

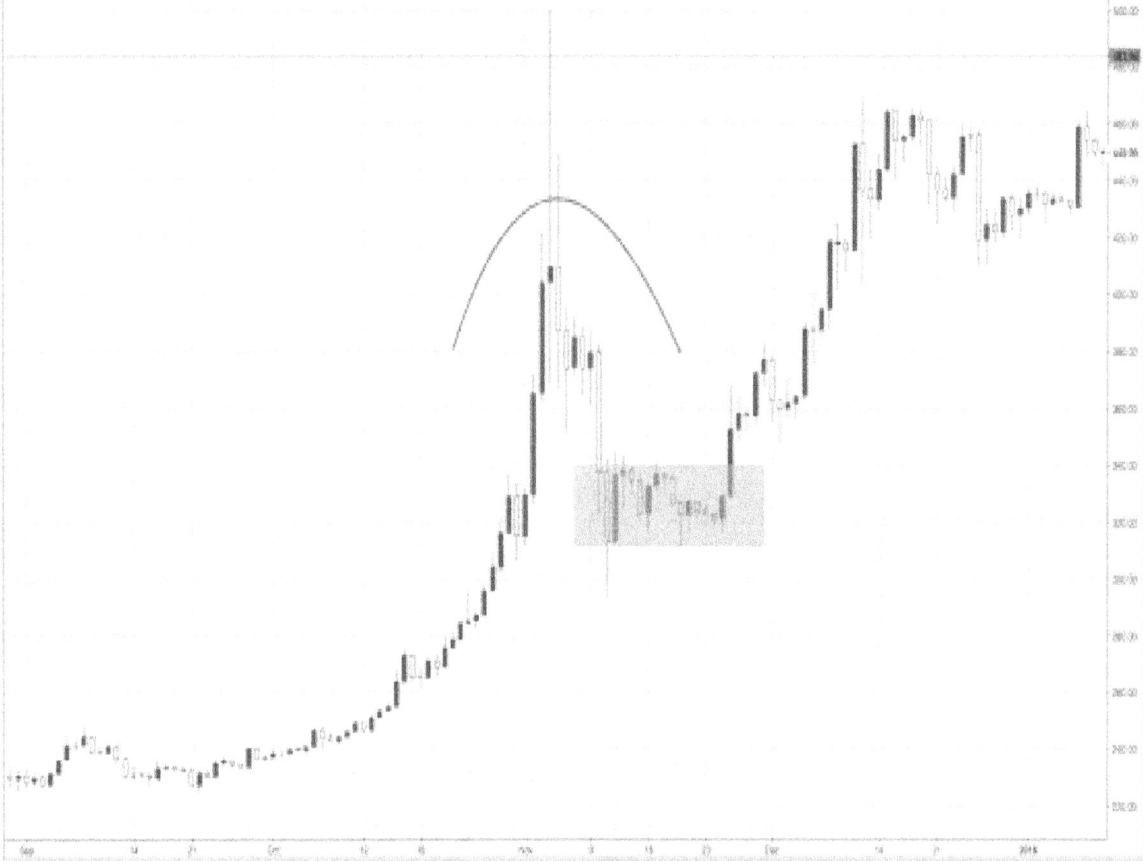

Trading Volume

Mistake 3: Not factoring volume into technical analysis

Another technical factor to take into account is the trading volume at a particular point in the chart. Ideally we want to see significant volume for upward trends, and lower volume for downward trends. If we see a downward trend accompanied by large volume, we can assume that this is not a weak trend and the price will continue to fall. Similarly, if we see volume is steadily decreasing on an upward trend, then this trend is likely coming to an end in the near future.

Limitations of Technical Analysis

Technical Analysis is just one tool that a trader needs in his arsenal. It is absolutely not the be all, end all of trading. Think of it as a guideline to making money, rather than a direct pathway.

The biggest factor is that we just don't have that much data available on the cryptocurrency market. Bitcoin has only been trading for 7 years now, and most other cryptocurrencies for less than 3. Unlike stocks where we have data for tens of years for individual stocks and the market as a whole.

Sometimes, if you dive too deep into the technical side of trading, you lose your instincts and even your common sense. Even if your charts are saying hold, you should probably sell if your position is up 100% over the past 3 days. After all, what goes up, must come down. Developing solid trading instincts is something that does take time, but the more trades you make, you'll start to subconsciously notice things.

Remember, if you are unsure of a trade based on your analysis, look at the bigger picture and add another timeframe to your chart to see if the same patterns emerge.

Trading Mindset/Trading Psychology

One of the biggest hurdles new traders have to overcome is acquiring the mindset of a successful trader. This is even more prevalent in the cryptocurrency market because its sheer volatility allows the potential for large losses in addition to large gains. These losses can be demoralizing for even seasoned pros, but the important thing to remember is to know that these losses will come (professionals estimate a 55:45 win/loss ratio for even the best traders), and how to deal with them when they do happen.

Acquiring a successful mindset is the single most important skill a trader must possess. Moreso than any technical tools. We must remember that we as humans have our own built-in biases, and even delusions, and many of these will hamper our trading ability. So the following is a list of important mindset and trading psychology factors that you must be aware of if you're going to become a successful trader.

Why Paper Trading is Useless

For years now, common trading advice has been that you should paper trade (trade with fake money) to get a hang of reading charts and learning when to buy and sell. However, I think this advice is limited at best, and potentially harmful.

You need to make mistakes with real money on the line, and you need to learn from these mistakes. Your brain and emotions simply don't react the same way if you know, deep down, that any losses you make are just on paper. To put it simply. You need to lose money to truly find out if trading is for you.

From then on, it's up to you how you react to these losses. Are you freaking out and trying to recoup them as soon as possible? Are you up until 4AM trying to get back some of the previous day's lost cash?

If the answer is yes, then trading probably isn't for you. However, if you can accept that everyone has bad days, and learn to analyze your mistakes and decipher where exactly you went wrong, and most importantly, learn from them - you may well wind up as a successful trader in the long run.

Paralysis by Analysis

So, you've spent your time reading and studying charts, now it's time to go to CEX.io or your preferred trading website and deposit money into your account. So you do so, and begin looking at charts, and waiting...and waiting...but you just can't seem to pull the trigger. This happens to a lot of new traders, especially those who are naturally risk averse. You want everything to go perfectly and you want to start out on a good note. However, this is trading, and as previously mentioned, you need to make mistakes in order to get better.

This is also why you need proper money management in trading, because say you lose on 8 out of your first 10 trades (not uncommon by any means), you'll need to have properly managed your bankroll in order to be able to fight another day.

Knowing when not to trade

Mistake 4: Trading for the sake of trading

One of the more important qualities of a good trader is restraint. In other words, being able to understand that there are days where you don't need to make a trade. Maybe there are no obvious patterns appearing, maybe it's just a slow day in the market. Either way, you need to learn to take days off. This is good for preventing trading burnout as well, especially in the cryptocurrency market that is 24/7.

Accepting that the market is always right

One of our great cognitive biases as human beings, is believing we are better than we are at certain things. For example, are you an above average driver? I bet 90% of people will answer yes, but statistically, only 50% of people can be above average at anything, that includes trading as well.

What I'm getting at, is we often make excuses for our bad trades, such as the old classic "the market is wrong." The market will move in ways you don't expect, and if anyone had figured out a way to truly predict market direction, they would be a retired trillionaire by now. Your technical analysis will not influence the market, it will only help you make better decisions.

Accepting that you are wrong

Following on from the above point. The market isn't wrong, you are. You need to be able to accept that you will be wrong on many trades, even multiple trades in a row. Remember, judge yourself by your results, and not on any perceived "clever moves" you may have made. You will always have losers, but you need to be able to take a step back and accept this in order to move forward.

Taking Intermediate Profits

If your profits are only on paper, you haven't made squat. You need to convert some of your gains back to fiat from time to time. Taking profits helps you mitigate your need to even more money on paper, which leads to greed taking over, which inevitably leads to losing money in the long run. If you enter a trade at $70, with a plan to exit at $80 because you see resistance there, then exit at $80. Don't let the coin go to $80 and then revise your plan and hope it goes to $100. There is no greater force that turns winning trades into losers, than that of greed.

Survivorship Bias

In my original book *Cryptocurrency: Beginners Bible* I talked about survivorship bias, and how seemingly everyone had made money with cryptocurrency. Well this is because winners speak up, and losers stay quiet. If you spend any time in the trading community, you'll be constantly surrounded by stories from traders who turned $300 in $50,000 in just a few weeks. Or a 19 year old kid from Russia who made $200 million in under a year. Of course success stories exist, but there doesn't mean there aren't as many, and in the case of trading, even more silent parties who lost money trading cryptocurrency. So the lesson here is to only measure yourself against yourself. If you're making continuous profits, then you're doing something right.

Recency Bias

You're only as good as your last trade is something that many traders suffer from, especially if they have a run of losers. This leads to negative mental energy, and a loss of confidence in oneself. What you need to learn to do, is not focus on these losses, but look at the bigger picture. Instead of focusing on your next trade, focus on your next 100 trades. By focusing on the next 100 trades, you remain committed to your trading fundamentals as opposed to chasing short term results and dopamine hits.

How to buy Cryptocurrency

Assuming you don't currently own any cryptocurrency, you'll need to buy some before you begin trading. The following is the most beginner friendly exchange for anyone looking to buy Bitcoin, Ethereum or Litecoin in exchange for fiat currency.

Coinbase

Coinbase represents the most simple way to buy Ethereum for those living in the US, Canada, the UK and Australia, in exchange for your local fiat currency. Based out of the US and regulated by the SEC, Coinbase is undoubtedly the most trustworthy cryptocurrency exchange out there today. Rates are competitive with the other major cryptocurrency exchanges, and the verification requirements are solid without being a hassle.

Currently Coinbase supports both wire transfers and purchases by debit and credit card. Once you signup for a Coinbase account and verify your ID, you can buy Ethereum, along with Bitcoin and Litecoin, instantly with your debit or credit card.

You can also store your cryptocurrency in Coinbase's vault system. If you do this, you will have to pass 2 factor authentication in order to spend it. This is one step more secure than simply leaving it on the exchange, but still is not as secure as offline storage option such as MyEtherWallet.

Another advantage of Coinbase is that they have a fully functional mobile app that allows the buying and selling of cryptocurrency on the go.

Now, as a special bonus to you - if you sign up for Coinbase using this link, you will receive $10 worth of free Bitcoin after your first purchase of more than $100 worth of Bitcoin, Ethereum or Litecoin.

http://bit.ly/10dollarbtc

Once you have purchased your Ethereum, there are a number of other exchanges I recommend if you want to trade Ethereum, many smaller cap cryptocurrencies do not allow for direct exchanges with fiat currency like USD, so you'll have to buy Bitcoin or Ethereum from Coinbase first, then exchange that for the other cryptocurrencies.

7 Common Cryptocurrency Trading Myths

Mistake 5: Believing any of these myths

1. **Cryptocurrency Trading Isn't Regulated therefore isn't safe**

This is one of the oldest cryptocurrency myths that still lingers around the market today. Cryptocurrency trading may not be regulated in the same way traditional securities trading is, but that doesn't mean the exchanges don't follow regulations. Coinbase and GDax are both registered in the United States and therefore need to comply with SEC guidelines. Other exchanges need to comply with their local jurisdictions as well.

2. **You need to know everything about blockchain technology to trade cryptocurrency**

Knowing the ins and outs of the coin you're trading might be helpful, but it's certainly not essential. In fact, an argument could be made that it is more beneficial *not* to know that much about your coin, to avoid making an emotional attachment.

Keeping up to date on cryptocurrency market news as a whole is advisable however. The two best sources for unbiased cryptocurrency news are.

http://coindesk.com

http://cointelegraph.com

3. **You need to know every single chart pattern every recorded**

You'd be much better off knowing the basics well, then having a broad but limited knowledge of hundreds and hundreds of different chart patterns. This is especially true when starting out, as you'll start to see patterns everywhere, even when they really aren't there, and as a result - make poor trades.

4. **Leaving your coins on an exchange is perfectly safe**

Exchanges are centralized, and therefore, are vulnerable to security exploits and hacks. From Mt. Gox in 2014 (which was handling 70% of the world's bitcoin transactions at the time) to Bitfinex in 2016, exchange hacks do happen. It's best to transfer any funds you are not using at the time to a safe, offline storage solution like a paper or hardware wallet.

5. **You should follow one person/one source's cryptocurrency trading tips**

Following a single person's advice is a good way to lose money, even if that person themselves is profitable, because there will be a delay in their trades and your trades. This means your margin will be lower, and thus you are less likely to make consistent profits over time.

A compounding factor to this is paid trading advice or paid newsletter subscriptions. These are often nothing more than pump and dump schemes by those running them. Unfortunately, as much of the cryptocurrency world is still unregulated, these schemes often go unpunished.

6. You should try to hit a home run with every trade

An important part of trading is knowing *when* to take profits. The newbie trader often mistakes the critical mistakes of going for just that extra 1 or 2% more, which often never appears and suddenly your gains have quickly turned into losses.

7. You can act as a perfect trader if you just learn the fundamentals

Unfortunately, as humans we have these little things called emotions. Fear, excitement, greed, all of these play a big part in our trading mindset and our subsequent trading actions. Mastering your emotions is a huge part of being a successful trader, and we'll look into this in more depth later on this book in the trading mindset and trading psychology section.

Best Cryptocurrency platforms for traders

Cex.io or http://bit.ly/cexsatoshi

With trading fees ranging between 0.1% and 0.2% per trade, CEX.io has some of the lowest fees in the crypto trading sphere. An added bonus on zero deposit fees for bank transfers and cryptocurrency deposits makes this a favorite among crypto traders.

Bitfinex

Bitfinex offers the best liquidity of any cryptocurrency exchange on the market today. They also offer margin trading. Their fees are slightly higher than Cex.io, and the tiers needed to access lower fees are also higher. But Bitfinex still remains one of the premier cryptocurrency exchanges for trading today.

GDax

GDax is a subsidiary of Coinbase, so falls under the same SEC regulations a Coinbase does. The ease of transfers from Coinbase to GDax make it preferable to those who would rather keep their funds all on one single web ecosystem. Fees are slightly higher than both Cexio and Bitfinex, but the ease of transfers may outweigh these higher fees for some traders. GDax fees range from 0.1% to 0.25% for "takers" (buyers) 0% fee for "makers" (sellers).

Poloniex

Poloniex offers a wider range of cryptocurrencies than other exchanges listed here. So if you're looking at trading some lower cap altcoin pairs, then Poloniex might be the best option for your trading.

Coinigy

Based out of Wisconsin, Coinigy is a rather interesting concept in that it's not an exchange itself. But a desktop application that gives you access to 45 different cryptocurrency exchanges from a single account. They also have 75 different technical indicators available. Although the interface might be overwhelming at first for new traders, more experienced traders may enjoy the sheer range of options available. Their pro account costs $15/month and allows for unlimited trading with no additional fees, which is extremely cheap if you plan on trading at high volumes. They also have an Android app if you want to trade on the go. At $15/month the expense is worth it, even for a novice trader because the charting features by themselves are extremely helpful if you're just starting out.

Mistake 6: Trading on the Wrong Exchange

Where not to trade cryptocurrency

You should stay away from any exchanges that could potentially be closed down by government regulators, these include Chinese exchanges. I would also not recommend Coinbase for trading, as the fees are higher than the other exchanges listed, however for a first time buyer, Coinbase is still the most accessible cryptocurrency exchange.

Where to store your cryptocurrency - Wallets & Cold Storage

Mistake 7: Storing your cryptocurrency on an exchange

Once you've successfully bought some cryptocurrency, be it Bitcoin, Ethereum or another altcoin, you'll need somewhere to safely store it.

Your cryptocurrency wallet is akin to a regular fiat currency wallet in the sense that you can use it to spend money, in addition to seeing exactly how much money you have at any given time.

However cryptocurrency wallets differ from fiat currency wallets because of the technology behind how the coins are generated.

As a reminder, the way the technology works means your cryptocurrency isn't stored in one central location. It is stored within the blockchain. This means there is a public record of ownership for each coin, and when a transaction occurs, the record is updated.

You can store your cryptocurrency on the exchange where you bought it like Coinbase or Poloniex, it is advisable not to do this for a number of reasons.

1. Like any online entity - these exchanges are vulnerable to hacking, no matter how secure they are - or what security measures they take. This happened with the Mt. Gox exchange in June 2011

2. Your passwords to these exchanges are vulnerable to keyloggers, trojan horses and other computer virus type programs

3. You could accidentally authorize a login from a malicious service like coinbose.com (example) instead of coinbase.com

Cold storage refers to any system that takes your cryptocurrency offline. These include offline paper wallets, physical bearer items like physical bitcoin or a USB drive. We will examine the pros and cons of each one.

Cryptocurrency wallets have two keys. A public one, and a private one. These are represented by long character strings. For example, a public key could be 02a1633cafcc01ebfb6d78e39f687a1f0995c62fc95f51ead10a02ee0be551b5dc - or it could be shown as a QR code. Your public key is the address you use to receive cryptocurrency from others. It is perfectly safe to give your public key to anyone. Those who have access to you public key can only deposit money in your account.

On the other hand, your private key is what enables you to send cryptocurrency to others. For every transaction, the recipient's public key, and the sender's private key are used.

It is advisable to have an offline backup of your private key in case of hardware failure, or data theft. If anyone has access to your private key, they can withdraw funds from your account, which leads us to the number one rule of cryptocurrency storage.

The number one rule of Cryptocurrency storage: Never give anyone your private key. Ever.

Therefore, with your trading funds, it's advisable to keep any excess funds offline, a hardware wallet is an ideal way to do this because unlike a paper wallet, it is much simpler to transfer your funds between the hardware wallet and your computer in order to fund your trading account.

Paper Wallets:

Paper wallets are simply notes of your private key that are written down on paper. They will often feature QR codes so the sender can quickly scan them to send cryptocurrency.

Pros:

- Cheap - all you need a printer and some paper

- Your private keys are not stored digitally, and are therefore not subject to cyber-attacks or hardware failures.

Cons:

- Loss of paper due to human error

- Paper is fragile and can degrade quickly in certain environments

- Not easy to spend cryptocurrency quickly if necessary - not useful for everyday transactions

Recommendations:

It is recommended you store your paper wallet in a sealed plastic bag to protect against water or damp conditions.

If you are holding cryptocurrency for the long-term, store your paper inside a safe deposit box.

Ensure you read and understand the step-by-step instructions before printing any paper wallets.

Bitcoin:

http://bitaddress.org

http://bitcoinpaperwallet.com

Ethereum & ERC 20 tokens:

http://myetherwallet.com/

Litecoin:

https://liteaddress.org/

Hardware Wallets

Hardware wallet refer to physical storage items that contain your private key. The most common form of these are encrypted USB sticks.

These wallets use two factor authentication or 2FA to ensure that only the wallet owner can access the data. For example, one factor is the physical USB stick plugged into your computer, and the other would be a 4 digit pin code - much like how you use a debit card to withdraw money from an ATM.

Pros:

- Near impossible to hack - as of the time of writing, there have been ZERO instances of hacked hardware wallets

- Even if your computer is infected with a virus or malware, the wallet cannot be accessed due to 2FA

- The private key never leaves your device or transfers to a computer, so once again, malware or infected computers are not an issue

- Can be carried with you easily if you need to spend your cryptocurrency

- Transactions are easier than with paper wallets

- Can store multiple addresses on one device

- For the gadget lovers among you - they look a lot cooler than a folded piece of paper

Cons:

- More expensive than paper wallets - starting at around $60

- Susceptible to hardware damage, degradation and changes in technology

- Different wallets support different cryptocurrencies

- Trusting the provider to deliver an unused wallet. Using a second hand wallet is a big security breach. Only purchase hardware wallets from official sources.

The most popular of these are the Trezor (bit.ly/GetTrezorWallet) and Ledger Nano S wallets. For altcoins that are not supported by these wallet, you can create your own encrypted USB wallet by following online tutorials.

Money Management while trading

Mistake 8: Not having a money management game plan

One of the most overlooked, but undoubtedly most important skills while trading is learning how to manage your bankroll.

You can think of trading cryptocurrency as akin to playing poker in this respect. If you put 50% of your holdings into one hand, then it only takes 2 losing hands in a row to wipe you out.

What's more is, when you lose money, you need to make more on your next trade in order to get back to your initial position. For example, if you lose 50% on one trade, you need to make 100% back on your next trade to break even. That's why trading with only a small amount of your holdings on a single trade is the smart way to go.

So no, you should never go "all in" on one single trade, no matter how much of a sure thing you think it is. The higher % of your total holdings you use for an individual trade, the higher your overall risk. In fact, the reason so many traders is that they don't anticipate losing a number of trades in a row. The holds true no matter how good you are at identifying chart patterns, or any other learned trading skill. Without proper money management, you will eventually go broke.

So let's just numbers. Because of the high risk element of trading cryptocurrency, I personally recommend that you do not risk more than 1-2% of your account on a single trade. The more active trades you are making at one time, the lower risk per trade should be. When you are starting out, I advise you risk no more than 0.5% of your account for your initial trades. This sounds low, but big dips do happen, and these can add up quickly, therefore we want to lower our risk as much as possible.

One more thing, cryptocurrency trading is a cash only undertaking. Under no circumstances should you borrow money from family, friends or financial institutions to trade. You don't want to start your trading career already owing people money, this has a huge negative effect on your state of mind and will cause you to make bad trades.

Risk/Reward Ratio

This is a vitally overlooked factor in trading. As we previously mentioned, if you lose 50% on one trade, you have to make up 100% on the next trade in order to break even. Therefore, you should enter all trades with a reward:risk ratio of at least 2:1. In other words, you must expect to make at least twice what you are willing to lose on the trade, because this will cover your losses from losing trades in the future. For example, if you are willing to lose $100 on a trade, you must be trying to gain $200 from that same trade. A higher reward:risk ratio allows you to have more losing trades, because your higher profits from winning trades make up for your losses on losing ones.

How many trades should you have open at once?

This is largely dependent on how much time you can spend looking at charts per day, but generally, you shouldn't have more than 5 or 6 open trades at a time. When you're starting out then one or two will be enough to cause your brain to work overtime. Remember to set stop losses if you want to manage multiple trades at once.

Which cryptocurrencies should you trade?

That's entirely up to you, however you should beware of coins with very low market caps and liquidity levels, as these are more susceptible to market manipulation and organized pump and dumps from nefarious parties.

I would recommend everyone start out with Bitcoin, purely because the market has the most liquidity.

Keeping a Trading Journal

Now, I'm not talking about a trading diary where you complain about your week's trading woes. I'm talking about logging your trades in an excel spreadsheet or a google doc. You can learn so much just from looking at your past trades, and you'll learn a hell of lot more from your losers than you will your winners.

As a thanks for downloading this book, I've including a handy trading journal for you to log you trades.

You can download the free spreadsheet at http://bit.ly/SatoshiTradingSpreadsheet

What causes price movements?

We have to remember here, that we are trading cryptocurrencies and not traditional stocks, and as such, the metrics for determining price are different.

The big difference is that there is limited fundamental analysis we can do on a coin when compared to traditional stocks. For example, we don't have earnings reports to look at or quarterly profit/loss statements. We also don't have to be concerned with potential mergers occurring between cryptocurrencies. Apart from, having a working product already, how fast the transaction fees are and scalability of the project, there really isn't much in the way of fundamental analysis. Both of these factors are more important for long term investing than they are for short term trading.

Market Sentiment

Overall market factors play strongly in the growth of individual cryptocurrencies. We are dealing with a singular market after all. For example, when Mt. Gox was hacked in 2014, and 850,000 Bitcoin were stolen, the entire market dropped as a result.

The second part of this equation is how mainstream media often misreports cryptocurrency price movements, being all too quick to cite a "plunge" or "crash". It's now getting to the report where media reports citing a "crash" happen on days where the price is still UP over the previous 24 hours.

Bitcoin's network effect is now so strong that many mainstream sources see Bitcoin as the be all, end all of cryptocurrency. Remember, buy the rumor, sell the news.

Bitcoin's price

The cryptocurrency market is still largely in its infancy, and as such, news regarding Bitcoin still greatly affects the market as a whole. At the time of writing, Bitcoin makes up roughly 56% of the overall cryptocurrency market cap, so any major Bitcoin price movements are reflected in the market as a whole. So even if you're trading smaller altcoins, it's wise to keep tabs on the price of Bitcoin as well.

Some commentators make the claim that Bitcoin and altcoin prices are inversely related, so if Bitcoin goes up, altcoins go down and vice versa. Whilst there is some data that backs up this theory, it isn't the entire story.

99% of people's first entry to the cryptocurrency market is into Bitcoin, this is even more so for institutional traders who move into cryptocurrency, because Bitcoin has the most liquidity, and therefore is an attractive market to enter. Therefore new money coming into the market is usually followed by investors moving their funds from altcoins into Bitcoin.

Asia

Mistake 9: Overlooking Asia' influence on the markets

One area to watch from looking for news to potentially affect trades, is any news coming out of Asia, particularly China and South Korea. These two countries have the highest volume of trades between them, more so than the USA, despite investors having to pay a premium (many South Korean exchanges trade cryptocurrencies for between 8-10% higher than US or European based ones). Any government clampdowns on exchanges or changes in legislation regarding cryptocurrency, is bound to have a negative effect on price. An example of this was the temporary ban on Chinese citizens investing in ICOs, which caused market prices to drop sharply. This was further compounded by the South Korean Financial Services Commission taking the same steps.

Stop Loss/Stop Limit Orders

Mistake 10: Not utilizing stop loss/stop limit orders

Stop loss and stop limit orders are both risk management tools that allow you to both prevent excessive losses on a trade, and also lock in any unrealized profits on an open trade. Both of these are relatively simple tools, but you would be amazed by just how many traders (usually the unsuccessful ones) fail to use them in their trading strategy,

A stop loss order is a level or particular price you set to automatically sell your position in a stock, or in this case a coin. For example, if you buy Bitcoin at $1000, you can set a stop loss order at $900, so that if the price falls to $900, you will automatically sell your position at that level, providing there is enough liquidity to fulfill it.

To use the second example above, say you make the same buy order for Bitcoin at $100, but it then increases to $110. You can set a stop loss at $105 to lock in your previously unrealized profits from this trade.

Effectively, you sell your position automatically once this level has been reached, which allows you to not have to monitor charts 24/7. This helps you in cases where a stock falls rapidly and prevents you from facing huge losses in open positions. The one drawback of relying solely on stop loss orders is that, if the volume is not there at your stop loss price, and the price continues to fall, your order will not execute and your position will still be open.

You can also use stop losses when shorting coins to prevent losses if the price increases after you place your short-sale.

A stop limit order is slightly different because you set both the maximum and minimum level you are willing to buy a particular coin. Let's say you want to buy Bitcoin at $95, but it is currently trading at $100, you can set a limit order so you automatically buy once it hits $95. But you can also set the order to automatically sell at $120 if it reaches that level. By doing this, you can step away from the computer, and providing the stock reaches those levels, the trade will execute automatically.

What you should set your stop loss at depends on your risk persona. Traditional trading advice recommends a 2% stop loss for each order, however with cryptocurrency's volatility, this may well be too conservative a measure and will result in excessive losses. I advise you to experiment for yourself and decide on your own personal stop loss point.

Note: For both stop loss and stop limit orders, you can employ a strategy of placing many smaller stop losses, which total up to your position in the coin - this prevents issues like a lack of volume to fulfill them. This isn't always necessary, but it worth doing as a precautionary step.

Margin Trading

Disclaimer: Margin trading is extremely risky, only do this if you can afford to lose everything you invest. Never ever short on margin in the cryptocurrency market.

If you're unaware of what margin trading is, Investopedia sums it up with this analogy

"Imagine this: you're sitting at the blackjack table and the dealer throws you an ace. You'd love to increase your bet, but you're a little short on cash. Luckily, your friend offers to spot you $50 and says you can pay him back later. Tempting, isn't it? If the cards are dealt right, you can win big and pay your buddy back his $50 with profits to spare. But what if you lose? Not only will you be down your original bet, but you'll still owe your friend $50. Borrowing money at the casino is like gambling on steroids: the stakes are high and your potential for profit is dramatically increased. Conversely, your risk is also increased."

Many cryptocurrency exchanges allow you to trade on margin, which is essentially borrowing money from the exchange in order to trade. Bitfinex allows for 3.3:1 margin trading, so for every $1 you have in your trading account, you can trade up to $3.3 on margin in the cryptocurrency markets. This is by no means the largest margin offered either, Kraken for example allows for 5X leverage on Bitcoin. BitMex, another exchange, allows for 100X margin, meaning you can literally borrow $100 for every $1 of your own money.

The reason exchanges allow margin trading is because the overall trade volume is higher, and therefore their fees are higher as well.

As a new trader, you should never trade using leverage. You are too inexperienced to be able to handle the potential losses that margin trading brings. Drops of 20 or 30% are not uncommon in crypto markets, and those drops are magnified when you are margin trading and can potentially wipe out your entire trading account.

Trading on margin also makes you vulnerable to flash crashes, such as in June 2017 when Ethereum fell from $360 to $13 for a brief period on GDax. Anyone trading on margin would have seen their funds wiped out in an instant.

Cryptocurrency Trading Bots

If you're not familiar with trading bots, they are automated pieces of software that perform technical analysis on stock, bonds or in these case, cryptocurrency. Ever since the boom in online trading, these bots have been synonymous with scams, pyramid schemes and other guaranteed money losers for those who use them.

The cryptocurrency world is no different, and I can safely say that the majority of trading bots on the market today are either completely useless or an outright scam.

Bonus Mistake 10.5: Believing "too good to be true" trading software or services

Cryptocurrency Bot & Trading Software Scams

CryptoRobot365

After defrauding hundreds of users, and receiving countless negative testimonials from those who never recovered their money, it's safe to say CryptoRobot365 should be well and truly avoided. To make matters worse, not only will you lose money, but your personal information may also be at risk.

The first warning sign is that this bot isn't registered with any regulated brokerages. The second being that although the software is advertised as free on signup, the actual minimum amount needed to have any access to the trading bot is a deposit of $250. The third sign being a fake "Best 2016 Performance Robot" icon on their website, when the site has only been registered since July 2017. The final nail in the coffin is that their testimonial page features a ton of fictitious testimonials using fake pictures and identities.

Unfortunately, as of the time of writing, the site still runs Google ads under popular keywords including "cryptocurrency trading bot". If you see it listed during a Google search, stay well away.

CryptoTrader.co

CryptoTrader.co's website opens with a man named Dave Richmond informing us that he can help us make $5,000 per day with his revolutionary new trading software. The software is apparently so good that he's turned 43 people into a millionaire last year! Notice any warning signs yet? Me too.

Like the above website, CryptoTrader.co also suffers from misinformation regarding how long the site has been functioning. The claims of making 43 people millionaire last year don't exactly hold up when the site has only been online for a few short months. The site also has no brokerage license or legal authority of any kind.

So with zero reviews on any independent websites, a website filled with a whole bunch of lies. An a frontman who appears to be a paid actor, CryptoTrader.co is definitely a no go as far as trading software websites.

Any person who approaches you with a trading bot

Occasionally if you hang out in enough cryptocurrency trading groups on social media or Telegram, someone will message me saying they have this great bot for sale at a surprisingly low price. If it looks too good to be true, it probably is. So stay well away from these low level scammers.

The only trading bot I recommend

HaasBot (http://bit.ly/HaasSatoshi) by HaasOnline is the only auto trading platform I recommend using. In a sea of scams and dodgy platforms, its nice to see a group with an ethical foundation.

The reasons for this recommendation are as follows: First of all, they refer to the operation as a trading platform rather than a trading bot. What they are actually selling is a software that numerous bots can be used with.

HaasOnline is completely upfront about what their bots *can* and more importantly *cannot* do. They don't make any vague guarantee about always beating the market like other bot or trading automation software does. Most importantly, they don't make any guarantees about monetary returns.

The software uses transparent technical analysis methods to perform trades. The bot uses this analysis to trade 24/7, and will add small amounts of volume needed to execute trades. There are also a number of safety features built in, to protect your investments.

Currently the bot supports over 500 different cryptocurrency pairings. Plus it is compatible with major cryptocurrency exchanges including Bitfinex, BitTrex and Poloniex. Where it may shine the most is with its built in arbitrage bot, which takes profits from the small difference between various pairings.

The team behind HaasOnline are based in the Netherlands, and there is a public figurehead in founder Stephen de Haas. In a discussion on popular Bitcoin forum bitcointalk.org, de Haas answered the questions "Can I get rich with this software?" in a frank manner.

"It's possible, but I can not guarantee this. As i stated before with speculation there is a risk involved. The main power of this simple trade bot is that it operated 24-hours a day. Meaning the bot will work for you when you are sleeping or working. This gives you the advantage of making more trades and possibly result in much higher profits."

Quality does come at a cost however, with the cheapest option being 0.09BTC (roughly $1000 at the time of writing), and the most expensive option being priced at 0.24BTC. However, this investment could be deemed as worth it by those looking to trade serious cryptocurrency volume, but can't dedicate 12+ hours a day to studying charts. The team also offers full, limited time refunds to those who use the software but for whatever reason do not like it.

Open Source Trading Software

There are a few open source platforms where developers have created their own trading bots for users to try free of charge. The two most popular of these are Gekko and ZenBot. Neither of these make any guarantees of profits, and were made more for experimentation than anything else. However as they are open source, and can be scrutinized by anyone, I'd thought I'd include them for those looking for a cheaper automated solution to their trading needs.

Trading Suicide

The following are moves that traders make that I consider trading suicide. Making any one, or more of these moves is generally a terrible idea, and **will lose you money** in the long run.

1. **Adding to a clear losing position**

Don't throw good money after bad. Let's say you've bought ETH at 300, and it's dropped to 270, but you're convinced it's going to rebound, do not top up your position. You may believe that by buying more at 270, your entry price averages out to 285, but you are unlikely to get back to this price before the stock drops even further. If you are clearly in a losing trade, close your position, get out, and live to trade another day.

2. **Focusing on single trades compared to long term profits**

Don't get attached to trades, especially bad ones. You may have thought you've done everything correctly, but sometime the market just knows better. Once again, get out, reset and live to trade another day.

3. **Checking prices of a coin after you've closed your position**

This is a subtle, yet deadly trading mistake that many losing traders make. It happens all too often, and leads to greed setting in for subsequent trades. Say you bought XMR at 180, and sold for 200, but you then see the price has gone up again to 215, and you start kicking yourself thinking "if only I'd held on a little bit longer", and you beat yourself up over your lost hypothetical profits.

The effect this has on your next trades is that it will cause you to hold onto positions for too long before closing, which inevitably leads to losses.

4. Chasing a coin past your initial target entry price

This is even more important if you're doing short term or day trading. You have a target entry price for a reason, because the charts say so. If for whatever reason you miss the entry price, then focus on another trade because your chances for profit has been drastically reduced.

5. Being impatient with winning trades, and being   too patient with losing ones

Sometimes trades take time to play out, sufficient buyer demand may take a few days or even a week to appear, but as long as the price is moving sideways, you can keep the trade open. If you see downward movement however, it's best to get out as soon as possible and limit your losses.

6. Not deciding if you want more fiat, or more cryptocurrency

Cryptocurrency is unique in the respect that you can still make a good trade in terms of dollars, but you can lose money in terms of actual cryptocurrency gains. The best way to combat this, is to decide which cryptocurrency(ies) you want to make the most of, and focus on trading with that goal in mind, rather than flip flopping between USD gains and crypto gains.

7. Not having a target exit price when you enter a trade

This is a surefire way to lose money. You need to have a target exit price or profit % based on your technical analysis, otherwise you will end up chasing gains for too long, and inevitably lose money. On top of target exit price, you should have a rough idea of how long you want to stay in the trade for.

8. Trading in an unstable mood

This includes if you're under the influence of alcohol or narcotics. If you're in a bad mood, then don't trade. Your emotions will get the better of you, and you make stupid decisions and cost yourself money.

Conclusion

So there you have it. The biggest cryptocurrency trading mistakes that new traders make - and you can avoid them and become a profitable trader.

So remember, pick a trading strategy, and don't deviate from it.

Don't panic trade, and trade when you're in an unstable mood. Trade rationally, removing all emotion from the trade (as much as humanly possible anyway).

Only trade cryptocurrencies you're familiar with. So it's best to start with the ones with most liquidity like Bitcoin, Ethereum and Litecoin.

And trade on an exchange with low exchange fees, so your profits don't get eaten up the more you trade.

Utilize the spreadsheet I included to help you track your trades and identify patterns in your own trading.

I wish you the best of luck, and most importantly, I hope you make a lot of money with cryptocurrency.

Thanks,

Stephen

P.S.

As a special bonus for buying this book. If you sign up for Coinbase using this link, you will receive $10 worth of FREE BITCOIN after your first purchase of more than $100 worth of any cryptocurrency.

http://bit.ly/10dollarbtc

Additional Trading Resources:

The following are additional resources for everything from charting to trading psychology. Note, the majority of these are not cryptocurrency specific, nor am I affiliated with any of the authors.

Top 10 Trading Setups Explained by Ivaylo Ivanov - Focuses on traditional markets like stocks, but the lessons can be easily applied to cryptocurrency. The book shows you how to recognize overall market patterns and how to approach each one of them.

Technical Analysis of Stock Trends (9th Edition) by Robert Edwards and John Magee - If you're going to buy one "encyclopedia" of technical analysis, make it this one.

One Up on Wall Street by Peter Lynch - Lynch famously beat the market 15 years in a row. Much of his trading advice holds true today as much as it did when the book was first released. Note, the paperback version of this book is cheaper than the Kindle version for reasons unknown

Cryptocurrency: What you need to know about taxes

to avoid a nasty surprise from the IRS

By Stephen Satoshi

Introduction

OK, so you've been buying or trading cryptocurrencies for the past few months or years and now you want to know exactly how this affects your tax situation.

To be frank, a year ago I had no clue either, so I did a research deep dive, contacted various institutions and people of note and found something fascinating...no one had any idea how it all worked! In fact, in 2015, the IRS discovered that only 802 people in the entire United States had declared any cryptocurrency related gains or losses on their tax returns. This has led to the IRS demanding Coinbase hand over customer records, which we will expand on later on in this book.

Fortunately, in the past 12 months we have had some concrete developments in cryptocurrency tax laws. Now we have the ability to at least construct an outline as to how this all works, and what exactly you are liable for when buying and trading cryptocurrencies.

I should note this is **not** tax advice. Everything expressed in this book is my own personal opinion and nothing more. Please contact a tax professional before you submit your tax returns.

One more thing, the content here is focused within the US market, your local tax laws may well differ.

Anyway, let's get cracking shall we?

Stephen

Some important things to know at the outset.

Early data from credit monitoring firm Credit Karma shows that less than 100 people out of a sample of 250,000 filings, actually reported cryptocurrency gains or losses on their tax return. This amounts to just 0.04% of the sample size paying their cryptocurrency taxes to the IRS. While obviously not all of those doing the filing would have held cryptocurrency, it's safe to say the actual number is a little higher than 0.04% of all American citizens. The latest estimates have around 7% of US citizens owning cryptocurrency in one form or another.

In another survey of 2,000 cryptocurrency owners, 57% said that they realized gains on their coins, but an even higher number (59%) stated that they had not reported any gains or losses to the IRS.

This combined with other factors like online tax providers (such as TurboTax) not integrating cryptocurrency taxation shows up that it's not just the citizen who are behind on crypto taxes, it's the authorities and tax based businesses as well.

What this tells us is that people in general are confused about how exactly they should file their taxes for cryptocurrency and therefore, more education in this area is needed, and that's what I hope to be able to provide in this book.

Let's start off with the basics shall we? What class of asset does the IRS consider cryptocurrencies to be exactly? Well, you may be surprised to learn that cryptocurrencies are not considered securities or stocks. Therefore there are a large number of tax laws that do not apply to cryptocurrencies. But there are an equal number that do apply and make this is a rather complex issue. So if you're getting excited and thinking that crypto is "tax-free" then think again.

So what are cryptocurrencies considered? Well according to IRS note 2014-21, any digital currency, or in their own words "virtual currency" is considered "property" for tax purposes. It should be noted that at the time of writing, this is only official statement the IRS has made about cryptocurrency. Oddly enough, the Securities and Exchange Commission (SEC) made a contrary ruling in 2017 when they decided that cryptocurrencies *were* indeed a currency.

The IRS ruling means your cryptos can be considered business property, investment property or personal property. In practical terms, and the big thing to note here is that any gain or loss is recognized every single your exchange your property, in this case, cryptos, to purchase goods or services.

Therefore if you're somehow who pays with cryptocurrency frequently, then you may well have more tax preparation to do than someone who merely buys and holds, or exchanges their cryptocurrency for fiat. This can make for an accounting nightmare if you haven't kept track of your cryptocurrency purchases. So I would advise you to do that as a bare minimum going forward.

The reason for this is that the IRS considers this two separate transactions. The first of which is the sale of your coins, and the second of which is using the proceeds of that sale to make a further purchase. Therefore, if you've bought Bitcoin at any time before January 2018, then it has most likely increased in value, and thus you will have to pay capital gains tax on it.

Let's use an example. You spend $4,000 on furniture at Overstock.com and you pay using Bitcoin (Overstock was actually the first major retailer in the US to accept Bitcoin as a method of payment). Using November 2017 figures, we'll say that Bitcoin was worth $8,000 at the time of the transaction, so you spent 0.5BTC on the furniture.

Now here's where it gets confusing, if you bought your Bitcoin back in early 2016 when BTC was trading for just $200 a coin, then you have a capital gain of $3,800 ($4,000-$200). Using the standard capital gains tax rate of 15% you have a $570 tax bill on your hand.

However here's where it gets even dicier. Even you spend your Bitcoin, or any other cryptocurrency within a year, then you may be subject to the short term capital gains rate of 39.5% (this rate is scheduled to fall to 37% in 2018). This is on the top of the sales tax you have already paid for the goods themselves, so you're essentially undergoing a double tax hit.

This has huge ramifications not only on a personal level (no one wants to be taxed twice), but also on a widespread cryptocurrency adoption level. And we haven't even begun to discuss how this affects day traders, how can make multiple cryptocurrency transactions per day. We'll expand on this point later on in this book.

We have to remember as well that this is the IRS we are talking about. One of the most powerful institutions not only in America, but in the entire world. The fact of the matter is this, if they want to find you, they will.

However, there are moves to make things easier for those who like to pay with cryptocurrency. A bi-partisan bill has been introduced by representatives that would only require you to report cryptocurrency purchases with a value of greater than $600. This makes more sense going forward, but it remains to be seen just how quickly this becomes written into the tax law.

How does my tax bracket relate to capital gains?

The formula for this simple for long term capital gains. So if you held your coins for a period greater than 12 months. It should be noted that these tax brackets are federal tax brackets, you state income tax level does not affect your capital gains.

People in the 10% and 15% tax brackets pay 0%.

People in the 25%, 28%, 33%, and 35% tax brackets pay 15%.

People in the 39.6% tax bracket pay 20%.

Hypothetical Scenarios:

Julie bought 1 Bitcoin on March 4th 2017 for $1000. She then sold her 1 Bitcoin for $3000 3 months later on June 4th. Therefore her taxable gain is now $2,000.

If she was in the 15% tax bracket she would pay $300 ($2000*15%).

If she was in the 25% tax bracket she would pay $500 ($2000*25%)

If she was in the 39.6% tax bracket she would pay a whopping $792 ($2000*39.6%)

But say Julie keeps her Bitcoin for 1 year, and sells on March 4th 2018 for the same amount of $2,000. Her capital gains now look like this.

If she is in the 10 and 15% tax she bracket pays $0

If she is in the 25%, 28%, 33%, and 35% tax brackets she pays $300 ($2000*15%).

If she is in the 39.6% tax bracket she pays $400 ($2000*20%)

So by keeping her Bitcoin for a year, she saves almost $400 in taxes for the exact same tranaction. So if you have no reason to sell (and remember, cryptocurrency is a long term investment so unless you literally need the money to eat you have no reason to sell), then you are better off keeping your coins for over 1 year to trigger the tax savings.

Now there is no way of telling if the price of cryptocurrency will be greater or less in one year than it is today. But if you have long term belief in the technology behind cryptocurrency, and thus its long-term viability as an asset as opposed to a short-term speculative vehicle, then it is well worth holding onto your coins.

What about if I sell for a loss?

If you have sold cryptocurrency for a loss at any time, this is of course deductible on your tax return. This is known as an "above the line" deduction, in the same way that interest of your student loan is deductible.

It should be noted that the maximal in capital gains losses you can deduct each year is $3,000. This is proportional to your income in the same way capital gains is. If you have more than this then you can roll it over to the next year until the remainder is cleared.

So for example if you buy Bitcoin at $10,000 and it crashes to $5,000, at which point you sell, then you have a loss of $5,000. You would be able to deduct $3,000 in this tax year and then $2,000 in the next tax year, provided that these are your only losses.

What if cryptocurrency is re-classified as a foreign

currency?

This is a perfectly plausible scenario. If this were to happen then any gains would be exempt from the capital gains tax, and more important there would be no more short term capital gains penalties. You would simply be taxed at your regular tax rate. This has a particular benefit to day traders who are currently at the mercy of short term capital gains rules.

However there are additional advantages in the case of transactions for goods and services. Under the foreign currency exemption for personal transactions (so not business or investment ones), gains under $200 are tax free. If cryptocurrencies continue to be adopted on a consumer level, where the vast majority of day to day purchases will be under $200, then this will be a big win for those who like to spend their coins.

The biggest issue we have in cryptocurrencies gaining foreign currency status is that because they are not minted or produced by a foreign bank - are they technically foreign at all? I would err on the side of caution for now, and go by the rules that the IRS has in place.

What if my job pays me in cryptocurrency?

This will only apply to a small percentage of readers, however that percentage is increasing at a rapid rate. Year by year there are more and more people working for crypto. This especially applies to those working on ICO projects who are paid in tokens by the founders in lieu of fiat currency.

Luckily, the way you calculate taxes for services rendered is pretty simple. If you sell goods or services (such as your own skills) for cryptocurrency, your tax basis is their fair market value at the time your cryptocurrency was received.

So if you received 10ETH for a project when ETH was $500=1ETH then you tax burden would be the equivalent of $5000. Obviously you should always keep track of the date you received your coins. You should also be consistent with which exchange you use, because choosing multiple exchanges for the benefits of better rates is unfortunately going to run foul of IRS regulations.

What if I haven't sold my coins yet?

OK, so assuming you haven't sold any coins, or traded them for any other coins. You have simply bought them for fiat and held. Then you would have zero tax events and you do not have to report anything to the IRS. Once you do sell or trade those coins, then it becomes a tax event and you would have to report any gains or losses made. So if you're a pure HODL'er, then don't worry about anything just yet, the IRS will only want to know when you sell your coins.

Let me make one thing clear at this point. **This is the only way to avoid realizing gains.** Any other suggestions are just patently false.

It should be noted that once you do sell them, it doesn't matter if you keep the money on an exchange or if you cash it out to your bank account. It still counts as sold from the time of sale. So you can't get around the IRS by keeping your money in Coinbase for example.

What if my friend/family member/dog gave me cryptocurrency as a gift?

I would be willing to bet that cryptocurrency gifts were at an all time high last year, and that more people received Bitcoin, Ethereum or Litecoin in 2017 than in all other years before them combined.

What you need to be concerned with is the basis of these coins when they were purchased. Hopefully there has been a gain in the time when the gifter purchased them for you and when you received them.

The confusing part of this is if they were purchased for a higher price than their value when you received them. So in other words if you have inherited a loss from the gifter. In this case you can use the value at the time you received them, not at the time of purchase. This regulation leads you to have the best possible tax situation with gifting.

If you haven't sold yet then you don't need to worry, but this does affect you when to do decide to sell. So as unflattering and impolite as this may be, it's worth asking your friend their purchase date and purchase price of the coins that have gifted you. This will ensure any future filings are indeed correct.

Let's do a few examples to clarify this.

Steve buys 1 Bitcoin for his friend Mary at $1,000. By the time Mary receives them, they are only worth $800. So to begin with, Steve's basis is $1,000 in this situation.

Scenario 1 - Mary sells for at $1,200. As she has profited, she inherits Steve's basis of $1,000 and she has a capital gain of $200.

Scenario 2 - Mary sells at a loss for $600. She cannot inherit Steve's basis so uses her own of $800 so her capital loss is $200.

Scenario 3 - Mary sells for $900. She still cannot inherit Steve's basis and a loss, so she uses her own of $800. Therefore her capital gain is $100, however as it is less than Steve's basis, it does not have to be reported as a gain or a loss.

The sale can be disregarded in this case, because there is no gain from the initial basis. This is all very confusing, which is why it is vital that you get the purchase price and purchase date from whoever gifted you the coins.

What if you are the gifter?

Like other gifts, giving cryptocurrency as a gift is not a taxable event because the recipient inherits the tax basis. So don't worry if you bought Bitcoin or Ethereum for your family and friends this holiday season, you're in the clear. Of course if you exceed the gifting limit ($14,000 for 2017 tax year) then obviously you will have to file. Note that if you are married and you and your spouse file together, you can give up to $28,000 or $14,000 per person.

There is also the lifetime gift exemption of $5.4 million but obviously that doesn't apply to the vast majority of readers.

How does the IRS know about my cryptocurrency?

Well this question isn't easy to answer, the short answer is that someone told them. Don't worry, there's no crypto snitches out there reporting your without your knowledge. There are a number of ways this can occur.

The most common is that the IRS requests the data from an exchange. They can do this with exchanges based in the US, and also exchanges based in countries which share tax treaties with the US. The biggest one of these is obviously Coinbase, and its sister site GDax, which is based in the US and is therefore subject to the demands of IRS.

They would report you gains in the form of form 1099-K. We discuss under what circumstances a 1099-K would be filed by Coinbase later on in this book.

The second way, and probably the most common way for the regular investor would be if your bank account was flagged for one reason or another. This is known as a Suspicious Activity Report (SAR) and many banks will file one of these because of cryptocurrency transactions. Banks tends to be cautious types so many times they will file a SAR based on frequent cryptocurrency transactions or transactions for large amounts. There is no hard number for the filing to be enacted but you can safely assume that any single transaction over $5,000 has triggered this. Obviously, the larger and more frequent your transactions, the more likely you are to be flagged. It should be noted that SAR filings are often done to avoid money laundering investigations so you shouldn't be worried if one is filed against you. Just pay the amount you owe and you can go on your way.

The third way is that you volunteer the information to the IRS yourself. Now there are significant penalties for failing to report income, so I recommend you report your gains within the appropriate reporting period. Now if you're behind, don't worry too much because the confusing nature of cryptocurrencies may well lead the IRS to be more lenient in this particular domain, but it goes without saying that you should file any back taxes as soon as possible.

The fourth and final way is indeed if someone reports you. If you're the ind of person who has a lot of enemies this is plausible. One lesson you should learn is to not brag or discuss large cryptocurrency holdings you may have, because people can and do get jealous, and as such, one may report you.

How to invest in cryptocurrencies tax-free

This is a big one that many investors overlook because it's not very well published, and your regular accountant probably isn't even aware of it. But the good news is its pretty simple and easy to execute even for a technophobe.

It is completely possible to add Bitcoin, Ethereum and other cryptocurrencies to your retirement portfolio such as your IRA. It goes back to the IRS ruling we discussed previously where cryptocurrencies are ruled as personal property. Therefore the IRS doesn't consider it to be "collectible" and as such there is no limitation in adding it to your retirement account.

There are two ways to invest in crypto using an IRA

The first of which is to use what is known as a "captive" IRA, so basically your provider will buy the cryptocurrency on your behalf and then you can store and access it as you wish. This is similar to how most IRAs work and if you use a financial advisor to handle your retirement affairs you will likely be familiar with the process. The drawback of this is that your account handler may not directly buy cryptocurrency and may instead buy an alternative form that is executed in cash, such as purchasing shares of the Bitcoin Investment Trust which actually trades Bitcoin at anywhere between a 20 and 50% premium in relation to its actual market price.

The second way of doing this is of course a self-directed IRA. If you already have an IRA dedicated to holding real estate or other alternative asset classes, you may be familiar with this one. The advantage here is that you will directly own your cryptocurrencies yourself. However these types of accounts are trickier to set up and therefore you must ensure you get everything right the first time round or otherwise you may get into hot water with the IRS down the line if everything is not in order.

To set up a self directed cryptocurrency IRA you must have your cryptocurrency stored in a wallet, in other words, not on a cryptocurrency exchange. However, this cannot be a personal wallet so you cannot use a hardware wallet like your Ledger Nano S for example. Thus you must work with your provider to set up a separate wallet which is purely for your retirement funds. I would seek advice from your provider to ensure everything is set up correctly.

The other option is that you can create a separate LLC for the sole purpose of holding the wallet and then be responsible on the balance sheet for all transactions in and out of the wallet. If you haven't done this before I wouldn't recommend it for a first timer, because the added complication of a cryptocurrency wallet can make it confusing to those without experience in the area.

FBAR Requirements

Now the FBAR applies to income stored outside of the United States. If you ever held more than $10,000 outside of the USA on a single day you are required to file your FBAR online. How this affects cryptocurrency is if you have ever had more than $10,000 worth of coins or cash on an overseas exchange, then you must file. This particular affects those who trade regularly on Binance and have held a significant amount of money on there.

OVDP & Streamlined Domestic Offshore Disclosure

Note if you suspect you are not compliant with these regulations for previous year,s you can file an IRS voluntary offshore disclosure and get back into the IRS' good books. The best way to do this is with the Offshore Disclosure Volunteer Program (OVDP), this program is designed to facilitate compliance with the IRS and the DOJ. The program is open to any US taxpayer with offshore holdings or financial accounts. The main requirement for this program is that you are not currently under IRS investigation. The reason for the previous necessity is that by being a voluntary program, you must not be "forced" to enter it, and if you are already investigation than that would constitute force. The standard OVDP application includes 8 years of tax return filings and 8 years of FBAR statements as well as other supporting documents.

The second one of these program is most applicable to most people. It's known as the Streamlined Domestic Offshore Disclosure. Despite it's strangely contradictory name, it deals with foreign accounts and foreign held money. Once again, contact an offshore disclosure attorney if you do wish to file.

If you have a significant amount and are behind on declarations, I would recommend investing some of that money and hiring a well experienced offshore disclosure attorney.

What about coins that were airdropped or I received as part of a hard fork?

Like most other cryptocurrency related tax issue, hard forks are a confusing one. According to Robert Crea from law firm K&L Gates "It's something new—it doesn't fit neatly into a dividend or stock split or even mining."

Crea's colleague Elizabeth Crouse then explained what this could mean for your tax liabilities.

"From the IRS's perspective, whenever you get something new you didn't pay for, it's accretive—it's income," she says. "When the Bitcoin Cash shows up in someone's account, that's probably a taxable event. The question is what's it worth."

As seen above, the main coin in question that we have to look for here is Bitcoin Cash (BCH). As a result of a hard fork, anyone holding Bitcoin on August 1st received an equivalent amount of Bitcoin Cash.

The question now is whether you would have to report this to the IRS and pay it as a capital gain, based on the price at the time of distribution (roughly $277 per BCH). Or the other scenario where you would only pay based on when you sold BCH.

The IRS is yet to make an official judgement on how exactly airdrops work though, and when contacted by various news agencies, simply referred back to their initial statements that conclude that cryptocurrency is considered property.

In this case, you would have to report your income based on the price of the coin at the time. In other words, just because your got your BCH for free, doesn't mean the IRS considers it to have zero value. In other words, it's a taxable event.

Now this gets dicey for those of your holding your Bitcoin in a Coinbase or GDax wallet because you would have received your Bitcoin Cash on January 1st 2018, when the value of Bitcoin was much higher.

The other big hard fork event, that will affect those of you who have been in the market for longer, is the July 2016 Ethereum hard fork when Ethereum holders received Ethereum Classic (ETC) as a result of the hard fork after the notorious DAO hack.

Then there is the case of air drops. Many coins over the past few years have airdropped into wallets on certain exchanges. Tron for example airdropped 500 TRX into Liqui wallets in September 2017. With this example, you inherit the cost basis of the "gift" at the time you received it. As many of these air drops had little value at the time you received them, it won't be an issue for the IRS. This is unlike BCH which did have significant value at the time it was distributed (approximately $277 per BCH), which is more likely to trigger a tax liability.

Of course, once again this only applies when you sell your coins. Simply holding them is not a taxable event.

Can I actually pay my taxes *in* cryptocurrency?

Is it possible to minimize your tax burden by paying in Bitcoin or Ethereum? Does the IRS accept crypto as a form of payment? Unfortunately the answer to both of these questions is a resounding no. The IRS does not currently accept tax payments in anything other than US dollars.

However at a state level, there may be some changes to this. For example, Arizona is the first state looking to pass a law that allows its citizens to pay state income taxes in Bitcoin as well as other sanctioned cryptocurrencies. This follows the lead of a number of municipalities in Switzerland which passes laws allowing their citizens to pay taxes in cryptocurrency.

If the bill passes it will be introduced by 2020 at the earliest so we're still a little ways off. Interestingly enough, the legislature states that Arizona would not hold the payments in cryptocurrency after they are made and would convert them back to fiat for their own use.

It is an encouraging sign though and we may well see other states follow suit in this respect. I would hesitate to think that federal allowance of tax payments in cryptocurrency is anyway close though due to the increasingly complicated nature of passing federal laws versus state laws.

What do I do if I haven't reported anything thus far?

OK so first things first, relax. Unless you have holdings ranging into 6 figures, it's unlikely the IRS or any other government agency is going to come kicking your door down.

Your best option depending on your holdings would be to contact a good tax attorney and accountant. If you do have significant holdings (6 figures plus), and you haven't been compliant for multiple years, I would urge you to spend more money and hire the best you can afford, because it will make the process a lot smoother going forward. The IRS is not an organization you want to mess around with and therefore you should absolutely do your utmost to be compliant.

Also, be wary of any company that promises cheap and quick offshore incorporation as a means of hiding assets or lowering your tax burden. Many of these companies can and will set up foreign bank accounts for you, but just because your money is going into a foreign account, does not mean you do not have to pay tax on it, as is the often misquoted information online.

Thirdly, everyone's situation is different, there is absolutely no one size fits all solution for this and thus do not believe everything you read on internet forums or social media. A good tax attorney and accountant is the only way you will truly get accurate information for *your* situation.

If you have low level holdings of only a few thousand dollars then you can still self report. Remember to keep track of all your crypto transactions, and if you haven't done so already, start doing this going forward.

Does taxation affect the price of cryptocurrencies?

This issue came to the forefront around December 2017, when a lot of first time crypto investors and traders realized that tax season was coming.

Therefore, there was a lot of speculation that tax season was actually affecting the day to day price of crypto. While some believed that many investors were pulling their money out of the market after December 31 but before January 31st to in order to pay their taxes, and spread their burden across multiple years. Others simply speculated that it was a coincidence and that the US market isn't the biggest player in the crypto world. However, a similar pattern has emerged for the past 3 years so the theory may well have some merit.

What is interesting is that this is actually a different pattern to the stock market which tends to do well in January as institutional investors reestablish their positioning as they move into the new year. Either way, it's an intriguing pattern to monitor going forward.

Needless to say, you can't let short term price fluctuations like this affect your long term investing strategy, so unless you are a day trader then it's best not to worry about minutia such as this.

What about ICOs - are they tax-free because they are used to raise capital?

While this would make sense, and would be in line with the 2017 SEC ruling that cryptocurrencies are a currency, the answer is actually no.

While conventional capital raising methods are considered tax exempt by the IRS. ICOs don't work in the same way. Therefore the proceeds of an ICO will be considered taxable income. The amount would be determined by the value of cryptocurrency received (in other words, the donation cryptocurrency rather then the new token) on the date the ICO ended. So if your ICO received 1000BTC and it ended when 1 BTC was worth $1000. You would have $1,000,000 of taxable gains.

The other thing to note is that unless you formed a corporation before you begin the ICO, you will be personally liable for the gains received. Obviously if there are co-founders like most ICOs then you are considered a partnership for tax purposes and you will be responsible for an equal share of the net income made from the ICO.

Therefore if you are a developer and are planning to conduct an ICO then you should definitely consider forming a corporation beforehand. Income will then be taxed at a corporate rate rather than a person rate which has far reaching benefits for the people involved.

One interesting thing to note is that by conducting your ICO earlier on in the tax year, you may be able to acquire some extra benefits such as being able to spend the proceeds on deductible expenses. This includes operating costs, salaries and other items like office rent.

There is a lot of speculation that forming an offshore company can have a number of tax benefits, especially when it comes to legally avoiding US taxes. Needless to say, offshore tax laws are extremely complex, depending on various factors such as the jurisdiction where your incorporated the company, your tax residency and a myriad of other factors. They are difficult for even a seasoned tax accountant to navigate so ensure that you have everything straightened out before you decide to go this route.

Beware of companies offering quick fix solutions like incorporation and bank account setup offshore, many of these companies will tell you that you will be completely compliant with US tax, but then you can find yourself in hot water down the line when it turns out there were certain things they *didn't* tell you in regards to your personal tax status. Often their advertising will use easy selling points like "0% tax rate", but it would be wise to investigate this fully before you do pull the trigger on any arrangement.

This is especially true if you reside in the US, then you income from an offshore company will still be subject to US taxation. Foreign owned companies will also have to deal with FBAR requirements that we previously discussed in an earlier chapter. You also have state taxes to be concerned with as your state will probably want some of your gains as well.

What if I make capital gains one year but lose the money the next year?

Here is a tricky situation, but certainly something we should all be aware of in the case of a market crash. If you make gains in one tax year, you will be required to pay them even if you make large losses the following year.

This can be troublesome in the case of a large year-long correction or bear market like we saw in 2015. There were a notable number of investors who made large gains in the prior year but as they expected this to continue, didn't take profits and kept much of their holdings in cryptocurrency. They went on to make some serious losses the following year and by the time their tax bill was due, they found they didn't have the money to pay it.

Obviously we can't predict the way the market is going to go, but we can take some steps to ensure that we aren't left out of pocket. The biggest lesson from all this is   that you should take intermittent profits for yourself no matter how good the market is doing, because trust me, you'll thank yourself the next year if the market does take a turn for the worse. Make sure you can cover any tax burdens, and don't leave it to the last minute to withdraw your money, because chances are a lot of people are doing the same thing, and thus it could cause a short term dip.

There are some exceptions to the rule but these will be made on an individual basis by the IRS themselves. So if this does apply to you, and you believe you could qualify for one, I recommend speaking with an accountant and seeing what can be done about your situation.

How are my cryptocurrencies taxed if I mined them?

Yet another area in which there is no real hard legislature right now is in the field of cryptocurrency mining. The IRS has made one ruling on this in Notice 2014-21 Q9 which states that anyone who mines cryptocurrency is "subject to self-employment tax on income derived from those activities."

In terms of how much your mined cryptocurrency is actually worth, the official IRS ruling right now is that each coin mined is given the value that it had when it was awarded on the blockchain itself. In other words, the value on the day it is mined, is the basis for that coin going forward.

For example, if you mine 1 Bitcoin when the value of BTC is $500, then its basis going forward is $500. So if you then sell it for $700 a year later, then your capital gains is $200.

When it comes to the subject of expenses and electricity, mining expenses are deductible if you have incorporated yourself into a mining business. Obviously if you are a mining business, electricity would be a significant proportion of your monthly expenses and therefore there is no reason at all why they would not be a legitimate deductible. It should be noted that you will also have to make note of the square footage of the room your mining rig is housed in, as this is often how electricity expenses are factored when there is a multi-use situation. It should also be noted that you cannot write off electricity for an entire room (like your living room) just because there is a mining rig housed there. Trying to do this is an easy way to get the IRS on your case. Other mining expenses such as depreciation of your mining rig and its parts would also be deductible.

If mining is just a hobby for you, you must still pay additional self employment tax on any amount earned which is greater than $400 in a single year.

Gains made from mining pools or cloud mining would be subject to the value of your payouts as well as money initially invested. Once again, consult a tax professional to get a better handle of the situation.

However on a strictly consumer level this is probably not a deductible. This is quite a gray area and I would recommend speaking to a professional for greater clarification on this subject.

Are crypto-to-crypto transactions considered "like kind"

exchanges?

This is where it gets murky, although the logic would dictate that these kinds of transactions are indeed "like kind" exchanges and thus would not be a taxable event, this officially is not the case for the time being.

Unfortunately the guidance from the IRS regarding this is over 3 years old now, when cryptocurrency and high volume cryptocurrency trading was far less common. So at the moment we will have to treat crypto-to-crypto exchanges as not being like kind and therefore every single trade will be a taxable event.

So what does this mean for your returns? It means that any gains or losses can be written off against each other for that particular year, but cannot be moved over to another year. So for example if you make $20,000 in capital gains one year, you cannot use these to offset a $10,000 loss the following year.

The other important thing to note is wash-sale rules. Designed so that traders do not fraudulently claim losses, this apply more to cryptocurrency than you might think. Wash-sale applies if you sell an investment at a loss, then re-invest in that same asset, in this case, the same coin, within 30 day of investing.

Let's do an example.

Say you buy 1 bitcoin at $20,000, it dips to $10,000, then eventually surges to $25,000. You sell 0.2 BTC at $5,000, which is a capital gain of $1,000 which you'd be responsible for short term capital gains tax.

However, if instead you sold your bitcoin when it hit $10,000 and repurchased it, you'd reset your cost basis to $10,000 and claim a $10,000 loss on taxes.

When the price increases to $25,000 and you sell your 0.2 BTC, it would be a $3,000 capital gain, but combined with your paper loss of $10,000, you'd still be looking at a $7,000 capital loss. For wash-sale rules to apply, all these trades must have occurred within a 30 day period of the initial purchase of Bitcoin.

Wash-sale rules currently only apply to stocks and securities, which cryptocurrencies are not considered as the IRS labels them as property. So in theory you could apply these to your tax return and benefit.

However, under regular tax law, you would have to prove these trades were done for some other purposes other than just to benefit on taxes. This is known as the Economic Substance Doctrine, so it is completely plausible that the IRS would not allow you to use these as a tax write off. The IRS uses this to fight against illegal tax shelters that long use this trick to provide additional tax benefits for their owners.

You can use the idea of market risk to argue to the IRS that these losses were sustained as a result of market volatility and nothing else. This is because the IRS considers you personal economic benefits at risk rather than just the potential tax benefits. Of course, any transactions over the 30 day period would not run foul of any of these rulings and thus you don't need to be concerned with them if that is the case.

The Coinbase Form 1099-K

We discussed this earlier in the book and now we'll cover it in grater depth. You may have received a form from the IRS in the mail within the past 3 months, this was likely Form 1099-K which relates to your cryptocurrency holdings which you **sold** in exchange for fiat value within the past tax year.

If you have received this it is likely that you have had a Coinbase account for a period longer than 12 months, and your sales of cryptocurrencies exceeded $20,000. The $20,000 number is based on federal law that third parties must report sales over this number to the IRS. Therefore, this is a form that Coinbase has to send to the IRS, as it strictly relates to transactions on third party networks. So in this case, it will only include transactions on Coinbase and its sister website GDax.

This form does not give the IRS an indication of your total cryptocurrency holdings, or those on other sites outside of Coinbase or GDax. Nor does it give the IRS access to your wallet address on those two websites.

The one thing to note is that the form relates to your gross payment amount. This particular relates to traders, especially day traders making many transactions. Therefore every single transaction is recorded and totaled up. In the case of Bitcoin, if you sold BTC at $10,000 twice - this would trigger the $20,000 threshold, and thus you may well have received the form, even if your net gains were well below this amount. This will also *not* take any transactions fees into account.

So if you sold your cryptocurrency for a loss, it would not take this into account. Therefore don't be surprised if the payment amount on the form is higher than your actual trading gains.

Let's do an example:

January   - you buy BTC at $8,000 and sell for $7,000 (a $1,000 loss)

February - you buy ETH at $500 and sell for $1,500 (a $1,000 gain)

March - you buy LTC for $1,000

The number on the form would be $8,500 ($7,000+$1,500), which is higher than your actual gains. This form only relates to the sale amount, so your purchase amounts won't even be displayed and thus the IRS does not have data into your actual trading profits.

It should be noted that if you have not received one of these forms but have been trading significant amounts, then it is your responsibility to file a 1099 to the IRS. You won't be able to use the excuse of "I thought Coinbase would do it for me" either, it's very much up to you to take the initiative in these kinds of dealing with federal tax authorities.

How to generate transaction reports on Coinbase &

GDax

If you're a frequent trader and you do make a lot of transactions, when you have to file your taxes, you'll need to make sure you note down every single one of these transactions. It will make it a lot easier to you square things away with the IRS.

Below is a step by step guide on how to find an accurate number of all your cryptocurrency transactions in the past year using Coinbase & GDax.

Instructions for Coinbase:

1. Click "Tools"

2. Click "Reports" in the sub menu

3. Click "+ New Report" button

4. Set Account to "USD Wallet…" and Time Range to "Last Year"

Instructions for GDax:

1. Navigate to the menu in the top right

2. Click "Accounts" in the sub menu

3. Click "USD Account" in the menu on the left

4. Click "Download Receipt / Statement"

5. Set Time Range to "Custom" from 01/01/2017 to 12/31/2017

How can you minimize your cryptocurrency tax burden?

So first things first, this applies to regular investors rather than frequent traders, who obviously will not be able to take advantage of many of the tax laws here. I should also note I am talking about legal ways to lower your overall tax bill. Not illegal ways to avoid paying tax.

The big one is to hold on to your coins for at least 12 months after you buy them. This will allow you to be in the long term capital gains bracket which will always be below 20%, whereas the short term capital gains will be taxed at the same rate as your regular tax bracket.

The second one is mainly for peace of mind purposes, but try to use as few exchanges as possible so it's easy for you to track all your trades. Being able to download your entire trade history from Coinbase or GDax is very simple, but other exchanges, such as EtherDelta, do not have any trade records at the time of writing. It's unlikely that the IRS will accept "well the website doesn't record trades" as an excuse, so try to use exchanges where you can have a record of all your trades where possible.

As previously mentioned as well, if you received coins as a gift that are now worth less than their value when you received them, you will be able to write some of these off as a capital loss. So ensure when you receive them you discuss with the gifter the date they were purchased and the value of the coins at that date.

Depending on your income bracket you may also be liable for an additional 3.8% Net Investment Income Tax. Consult the IRS website for further details.

Can you register yourself as a self-employed trader to get a better tax deal?

There are a number of advantages to being a self-employed trader in the eyes of the IRS. The main one being, if the IRS considers your trading a "business" then your gains and losses become ordinary.

Registering a trader is extremely difficult though and your registration must be renewed twice a year to qualify for the benefits. There are a number of advantages and disadvantages to doing this. The may disadvantage being that your losses are no longer deductible because this are considered part of your day to day business and thus regular capital gain rules no longer apply.

However, just being on Binance a lot is not going to cut it come tax season. So if you do want to register yourself I would recommend consulting a tax professional if you want to go this route.

What about altcoins with no official conversion to fiat

In the case of many altcoins that don't have direct fiat trading pairs, you would use the USD value of the fiat equivalent that you traded them for. For example if you bought 50XMR for 20 BTC and that 20BTC was worth $10,000 at the time, then officially you bought $10,000 worth of currency during that transaction.

This applies when you go to sell as well. It doesn't matter if the final sale was against another altcoin or not, the transaction will be recorded in US dollars. Obviously this represents a great difficulty for a lot of people, so if you have been trading frequently I would seek out professional help from a tax firm.

Were there any changes in the crypto tax laws between 2017 and 2018?

So as we previously stated, there has only been 1 official ruling on cryptocurrency by the IRS. This was back in 2014, and nothing much has changed since then.

So like-kind exchanges still apply, you will pay taxes on crypto-to-crypto exchanges when you eventually convert these to fiat. Obviously this implications will have more effect on frequent traders and day traders then your regular buy and hold investor.

There are new federal tax brackets, which will affect your capital gains and these are listed below.

Rates for Individuals in 2018.

10% - Up to $9,525

12% - $9,526 to $38,700

22% - 38,701 to $82,500

24% - $82,501 to $157,500

32% - $157,501 to $200,000

35% - $200,001 to $500,000

37% - over $500,000

Rates for married couples filling jointly

10% - Up to $19,050

12%- $19,051 to $77,400

22% - $77,401 to $165,000

24%- $165,001 to $315,000

32%- $315,001 to $400,000

35%- $400,001 to $600,000

37%- over $600,000

How are other countries dealing with cryptocurrency taxes?

While we wait for US tax law to evolve to being at a happy medium with cryptocurrency gains, it is interesting to see just how other countries are handling the problem.

Germany for example considers cryptocurrency to be foreign currency and trading in cryptocurrencies is considered a private sale. They also do not have any long term capital gains tax on cryptocurrency, so if you buy 1 ETH on June 1st 2016 and sell it for a profit on June 1st 2017, then you would not have to pay any tax on your gain.

Denmark is another progressive crypto country. In its goal of making the Nordic nation the world's first cashless state, cryptocurrency trades are not taxed and there is no capital gains on Bitcoin either.

In January 2018, the Portuguese tax authorities announced they would not be levying any taxes on profits made by trading cryptocurrency. The government of Belarus also announced that as of March 2018 there would be no taxes on cryptocurrency for its citizens for the next 5 years. This is to encourage the adoption crypto as well as to promote blockchain and smart contract technology. Serbia is another nation that is completely tax free for cryptocurrency profits, including profits made from crypto mining.

However, other countries are less friendly towards their citizens bank accounts when it comes to cryptocurrency, for example, in Germany the short-term (less than 1 year) capital gains tax can be as high as 46%. In France, the situation is even worse and this number can top 60% in some cases.

Then there's the rather bizarre case of the few select crypto millionaires who are trying to construct their own "cryptocurrency utopia" in Puerto Rico. By establishing residency on the Caribbean island, which is a U.S. territory, they are aiming to avoid state and federal taxes. Puerto Rico has become somewhat is a tax haven in the past decade due to no federal personal income taxes, no capital gains tax and favorable business taxes — all without having to renounce your American citizenship. Which makes it an ideal tax haven for any US citizen.

There are talks of many of these men building lavish mansions with their own docks and airstrip for private planes. These men include Bryan Larkin, a crypto billionaire who was one of the early adopters of Bitcoin mining with an estimated personal fortune of around $2 billion. Another notable figure is Reeve Collins, one of the co-founders of the controversial US Dollar tether, which is a cryptocurrency pegged to the value of the US dollar, used for exchanges between altcoins. Needless to say, the project is in the early stages still and many of the group spend the majority of their time drinking at hotel bars rather than building mega mansions. It will definitely be interesting to see if it ends up as a cryptocurrency utopia or if the opposite happens and it turns into a Lord of The Flies situation.

Conclusion

Well there we have it, I hope I've cleared up some questions and that you've come out of this book with more knowledge about the general cryptocurrency tax situation than before.

We've covered everything from capital gains and losses, to how mining cryptocurrencies is taxed as well as gifting. We've also gone over the different forms that are filed and the various ways the IRS will be aware of your cryptocurrency tax situation, so I hope I've been able to address the vast majority of concerns you had before buying.

Remember, everyone's personal tax situation is different, and there is no one size fits all solution, no matter what anyone tries to tell you. It should be noted that anyone trying to tell you that their one size fits all solution works for you, is probably just trying to get your money.

If you have a single take away from this book let it be this. The only person who will be able to help with your own situation is a qualified accountant or tax attorney. This is one area I would recommend paying more money and hiring the best you can afford, especially if you have made a lot of more with crypto.

I wish you the best of luck in your ongoing cryptocurrency journey. We all hope the IRS can get a better grip on the crypto tax situations as we go forward, but it may well be a few years before we get some better guidelines and more streamlined processes. In the meantime, just make sure you keep up with tax compliances and file on time every years.

And as always, I hope you make a lot of money with cryptocurrency and that it affects your life in a positive way.

Thanks,

Stephen

www.ingramcontent.com/pod-product-compliance
Lightning Source LLC
Chambersburg PA
CBHW081810200326
41597CB00023B/4207